# *The Elusive*
# MASTERPOINT

## CARL VANCELETTE

SQZ
SQUEEZE
BOOKS

*Cover design: Jay Cookingham*
*Interior design: : Jay Cookingham*

ISBN: 1-58776-159-9
ISBN 13: 978-1-58776-159-1

Library of Congress Number: 2006938860

. Bridge Book

Manufactured in the United States of America

VIVISPHERE
PUBLISHING
675 Dutchess Turnpike, Poughkeepsie, NY 12603
www.vivisphere.com (800) 724-1100

*To my favorite partner in bridge and in life - Claudia*

*Many thanks to my editors, Jody Latham, Brent Manley and Ron Garber without whom this book would have not been possible.*

# PUBLISHER'S NOTE

Most of us remember fondly our climb up the masterpoint ladder. That's because we've blocked out memories of the disappointment and embarrassment we felt when we made that same darned mistake yet again.

Carl Vancelette hasn't forgotten anything. And somehow, with every lesson he recalls for us, there's a laugh attached.

There is a commonly accepted misconception that you can learn only from an expert. Wrong! You can learn plenty from someone who has been through the same obstacle course that you have.

Learn. Laugh. Remember.

Another on-demand production.

Ron Garber
*for SQueeZe Books*

# CONTENTS

# PART VII

♠ ♡ ◇ ♣

P A R T   O N E
# The Early Days

Like many baby-boomers, I was introduced to bridge in college. My fraternity was a bridge-playing house. It didn't matter how much you knew. If you could hold thirteen cards, they would walk you through the rest. The only important thing was that you were a fourth.

I can recall many times settling down for an evening of serious studying in my room. I'd have soft music playing on the stereo, lights turned down low except for my desk lamp to facilitate concentration, texts and assignments all arranged and ready for some uninterrupted academic productivity, when one of the brothers would poke his head through my door, hold up four fingers and ask "Fourth?" And that was the end of that.

Bridge games would last well into the next morning, so whatever chance there had been of getting any studying done was long gone.

After college, bridge was forgotten. Marriage, a new job, and raising a family left little time for what I figured was only a college game anyway. They didn't play it in the real world did they? Then some friends of ours reintroduced us to the game. They had taken some duplicate lessons in their city's adult basic education program, and they thought it was something my wife Claudia and I would enjoy.

By this time, our two families were camping together on a lake in northern New Hampshire. While other families spent the evening around campfires, the four of us were crowded around our camper's cramped dining table playing bridge. We had to try duplicate, our friends told us. We had no idea what that was, so they found our local club game in the ACBL directory and dragged us off to our first game. It was eight tables at Pease Air Force Base in Newington, New Hampshire. Claudia and I can both remember picking up the first deal of the evening, and our hands were trembling we were so nervous. What was there to be nervous about? People were more than happy to see us come to their table and give them three tops.

No matter. We were hooked. There was no looking back. We had become duplicate bridge players.

♠ ♡ ◇ ♣

# CHAPTER 1
# Welcome To Duplicate

*Bear welcome in your eye,*
*Your hand, your tongue;*
*look like the innocent flower,*
*But be the serpent under 't.*
Lady Macbeth

I can still vividly recall our introduction to duplicate bridge. DUPLICATE! This was no longer just for fun. This was serious business. Errors became zeroes. Everyone in your direction had done better with your cards than you had. How embarrassing. Conversely, there were also tops. For my wife Claudia and me, there were unfortunately many more of the former than the latter. I'm sure our opponents eagerly anticipated the many gifts we handed out.

In those early days of bridge, however, there were some fellow novices with whom we actually managed to laugh at our gaffes. One couple, Joan and Al, had played bridge for years but not a great deal of duplicate. They got as much enjoyment from an evening out with friends as they did from any masterpoints they might win. I'll never forget the round we played with them one Friday night at the club.

After some friendly banter, we played the first board. TWO HEARTS, making two. Claudia, sitting North, changed the boards, but then Joan had a question about the other scores on the first board. Claudia took out the traveler to check. THREE NO TRUMP by South, down one. Both times! We were all befuddled until we realized we were looking at the slip for the second board- the one we hadn't played yet. I said we should call the director.

"Oh no," Joan implored. "We paid our money. Let's just put the slip away and play the board."

"Okay," I relented, "but we're sure not going to bid THREE NO TRUMP."

Laughs all around except from Al who was adjusting his hearing aid. We took out the following hand:

## DLR: NORTH    VUL: N-S

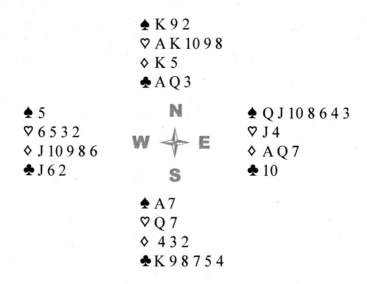

&spades; K 9 2
&hearts; A K 10 9 8
&diams; K 5
&clubs; A Q 3

&spades; 5
&hearts; 6 5 3 2
&diams; J 10 9 8 6
&clubs; J 6 2

&spades; Q J 10 8 6 4 3
&hearts; J 4
&diams; A Q 7
&clubs; 10

&spades; A 7
&hearts; Q 7
&diams; 4 3 2
&clubs; K 9 8 7 5 4

Claudia, sitting North, opened ONE HEART. Al, East, overcalled ONE SPADE. I bid ONE NO TRUMP. "THREE NO TRUMP," said Claudia confidently. I couldn't believe my ears.

"What are you doing?" I asked incredulously. "THREE NO TRUMP goes down one."

"I'm just being fair and bidding my hand," said my wife, the model of honesty.

Joan, who has one of the club's most infectious laughs, squealed with delight. The bidding, however, was not over yet. Al, oblivious to all of the turmoil, was still studying his cards. His hearing aid still wasn't adjusted, and he hadn't heard any of the discussion. "FOUR SPADES," he bid.

"What are you doing?" Joan asked him. "Have you lost your mind?"

"Double," I said thankfully.

When the debacle was over and we had tallied our 500 points, Al picked up his hand and looked at it sadly. "I'm sorry, dear," he said. "I guess I should have doubled THREE NO TRUMP."

There's more to this story, though. We were not the only plus on the board, nor did we get a top. By the end of the session, one South chose to bid TWO CLUBS over ONE SPADE, and North got to THREE NO TRUMP taking all thirteen tricks on a spade lead. One West led a spade and suffered the same fate. And one pair got to SIX CLUBS by North (how did they manage that?), making seven on a spade lead. Welcome to duplicate bridge!

♠ ♡ ◇ ♣

# C H A P T E R  2
# The Bridge Gods

*Concerning the gods, I am not in a position to know either that they are or are not, or what they are like in appearance; for there are many things that are preventing knowledge, the obscurity of the matter and the brevity of human life.*
Protagoras   490-420 B.C.

Maybe Protagoras was right, but I know one thing for sure. The bridge gods really do exist. My wife Claudia offers proof from one of the first regional tournaments we ever attended.

When we took up the game of duplicate bridge, we discovered a whole world of competition we didn't know existed. Just as there are tournaments at various levels for such other endeavors as chess, bowling, archery, and skeet shooting, bridge offered a whole array of events from sectionals and regionals to nationals. Vacations could now be combined with bridge tournaments.

The only problem with all of this was that, for me and Claudia, it wasn't just a partner sitting across the table, it was a spouse. Now you'd think that playing bridge with your spouse would be advantageous, wouldn't you? You could fine tune your system, talk about the hands after your last game, and spend hours that more casual partnerships wouldn't have going over your card, right? Oh no. This was your spouse, remember?

Criticism from me was always taken personally, and I had plenty of criticism to offer. After all, I had played bridge in college, and she was just learning. Thus, hostility was a presence always hovering just beyond the context of our game. Claudia and I have a wonderful marriage, and we almost never argue about anything…except bridge! Claudia's choice to stubbornly lead her own suit rather than the one I bid or to ignore some bidding sequence I have suggested for one that made more sense to her has precipitated numerous battles surpassed in intensity only by some of the most prodigious engagements in the Civil War.

We both read Roselyn Teukolsky's book *How to Play Bridge With Your Spouse (And Survive)*. Claudia devoured it one evening as she sat in the living room with me. "Ha!" she exclaimed after each particularly appropriate example in the book (there were many) and fired an accusatory look in my direction. "You see. He makes faces at her too."

"I try not to make them any more. I've been pretty good lately, haven't I?"

"I know you're making them inside. I can tell what you're thinking."

Along came the regional in Manchester, NH, and there it was that the bridge gods manifested themselves, demonstrating- to Claudia at least- that there is indeed justice at the bridge table.

On Friday night we decided to try knockouts for the first time. Friends had told us that knockouts were a much more leisurely form of bridge. You play 14 boards against one pair while your teammates play the same boards against another pair. You then compare results and play fourteen more boards. At this form of scoring, there is not the intense concentration on every trick that duplicate demands on both offense and defense. You simply try to make your contract or set the opponents. An overtrick one way or the other seldom makes a difference. Our friends were right. We survived the first round of the knockouts, and on Saturday we were one board away from earning our very first gold points. Here was the fateful hand. In first position vulnerable, I picked up:

♠: A 10 9 8 7  ♡: A Q J  ◊: A 9 8  ♣: K 10

I opened ONE SPADE in first position, and my wife bid THREE NO TRUMP, which at the time was our strong spade raise. I went to Blackwood and, off a king, settled into SIX SPADES after giving a moment's thought to SIX NO TRUMP. No, I reasoned, that would be a matchpoint bid, not a good bid at total points. Better to be in the safe spade contract. I got a heart lead, and this is what I saw:

♠ Q J 5
♡ K
◊ K J 10 7 5 4
♣ A J 6

♠ A 10 9 8 7
♡ A Q J
◊ A 9 8
♣ K 10

I won the king in dummy and took the immediate spade finesse which, naturally, lost. Back came a spade. Where was the queen of diamonds? A two-way finesse. I always got those wrong. Always. I thought about stripping the hand first. King of clubs, club to the ace, ruff a club, just to see what happened. I played the king and something-*something*- stopped me. No, I had to do the diamonds. Nine never? I led to the king. Nothing. Back to my hand and right hand opponent showed out! What now? In a blind panic, I ran all my hearts and spades and pitched...clubs! At the end I lost a diamond to the queen. If only I had played a second club, the queen would have fallen doubleton! The jack of clubs would have provided a resting place for my losing diamond.

Claudia said that on the King of Clubs my left-hand opponent had dropped a suspicious looking nine. I never saw it. I was thinking too hard about the finesse I would never take. At the other table, the bidding went ONE SPADE, TWO NO TRUMP, SIX NO TRUMP! A club lead gave them their immediate twelfth trick. There were four ways I could have made this hand: (1) Do the top diamonds first and save the club finesse for later. (2) Do the clubs first. What stopped me? (3) Finesse the diamond the right way. (4) Bid no trump. Incredibly, I had found the only way to go down. "Thank God that wasn't me," said Claudia.

I slept little that night playing the hand over and over in my mind. The caddy could have made that contract. Why hadn't I played the second club? Why?

Oh well, Sunday was another day and, as luck would have it, we were in contention for first place in the Flight C Swiss Teams. Going into the last round, we had 90 Victory Points, tied for second with another team. The first place team only had 97 points. Two other teams were lurking in the high 80's. We had to play the team with 87 Victory Points. Every deal was a partial, no swing to be found. I thought sure we needed to make something happen. In fourth position, I picked up:

♠: 8 7   ♡: A 9 6 5   ◇: A 7 6 5   ♣: 8 4 3

My wife opened ONE SPADE, and I said ONE NO TRUMP. She bid TWO NO TRUMP. THREE NO TRUMP I heard myself say. Down two. I had found a swing all right. That board cost us the match, which we lost 13-7. Amazingly, none of the other teams in contention did anything, and the team with 97 only got three points to tie for first at 100. All I had to do was keep my mouth shut and we would have won the event.

When Claudia extricated the cards from my death grip to examine my hand, she said "You went to THREE NO TRUMP with that? What if I had done that? Would I have ever heard the end? Ever?"

The ride home was unusually quiet. Normally I would be lecturing Claudia on some finer point of the game or other- a bid she had missed or some subtle error I thought I had seen in her play.

Kind of quiet, aren't you?" she asked. When I didn't reply, she smiled contentedly, looked out of the car window into the night and said with assurance, "There really are bridge gods, aren't there. They really do exist."

I thought back to whatever it was that had caused me to pitch a club from dummy in my slam hand and that had compelled me to bid THREE NO TRUMP. Was she right? Could it be? Nah.

♠ ♡ ◇ ♣

C H A P T E R 3
# The Fine Art of Balancing

*A little learning is a dangerous thing.*
-Alexander Pope

My wife Claudia and I had played about five or six sessions of duplicate bridge when some friends of ours convinced us to go to Toronto for a vacation and to play in the 1986 Summer North American Bridge Championships. This was quite a step, for we had only been playing duplicate for about a month. The first time we played, our friends had to drive all the way down from Vermont to take us to the club and give us moral support. I can still remember trembling at the first table when I took out my cards.

Actually the experience wasn't that bad. Finishing last wasn't as painful as we thought it would be. Our friends had finished average. "Wow," we thought, "average. Do you think we will ever be average?"

"Do you really think we're ready for the North American Championships," I asked my friend over the phone. I wasn't aware that the NABC offered games for all levels of players.

In Toronto, we played in the zero to five point game for three successive evening sessions. One time we even managed to finish average. We were thrilled. My clearest memory of those games was the shrill voice of Edith McMullin over the microphone constantly referring to us as THE BABIES. "Come on, babies, let's catch up."

On the fourth night, we had no idea how we had done. After the game, we took a walk around the hotel, and when we returned, our friends were standing by the posted scores. "Congratulations," Steve said. We had finished third! We were ecstatic.

Later, when I went back to the scoresheet to copy our scores, a pleasant man whom I later found out was Edith McMullin's husband, came up to me and asked how I had done. "Third," I said proudly.

"Good for you," he said. "Let's look at your scores and see if I can help you with anything."

He immediately picked out board 7. "Two diamonds by the opponents, making two," he said. "Uh uh. That's not good bridge."

"Why not?"

"You have to *balance*." He explained the fine art of balancing- not allowing the opponents two play a low level contract like TWO DIAMONDS.

Later at the tournament, I bought my first bridge book at the book display- *The Complete Book of Duplicate Bridge* by Kay, Silodor and Karpin. In it there was an extensive section on balancing with page after page of examples that showed when and how to balance.

Armed with this information after the National, I went back to our Thursday night club in New Hampshire ready to push and shove our opponents into unmakable contracts. Our first round was against a life master, who was a former state champion, and his wife- two of the many people of whom we were in awe at our club. In second position, I picked up this hand:

♠: Q J 10 8   ♡: J 7 3   ◇: Q 8 7   ♣: K J 6

The bidding went ONE HEART from the former state champ on my right. PASS from me. TWO HEARTS from his wife. PASS. PASS. I was ready. TWO SPADES I said fearlessly. THREE HEARTS from the champ's wife. I could almost hear the champ's thought process as he stewed over this development. How could she go to THREE HEARTS if she was only worth a TWO HEART bid the first time around?

FOUR HEARTS said the champ, as much to punish his partner as for any other reason.

"Sorry dear," said the wife as she put down the dummy. "I had the king of clubs hidden in with my spades. I'm glad he balanced."

The champ made an overtrick. I had turned a cold top into a tie for bottom.

"Nice going," my wife said.

"I was only *balancing*," I said. "I'm supposed to *balance*." I could see she didn't understand.

Undaunted, I took David, a friend of mine, to his first sectional tournament a few weeks later. David had played a lot of whist, but duplicate bridge was new to him. We had played in a couple of club sessions together, and as we drove to the tournament we went over the bids and conventions that we were using. I neglected to tell him about *the fine art of balancing,* however.

A ways into the match, we sat down against two Life Masters. I picked up this hand in fourth position:

♠: Q J 10 8 4    ♡: J 7    ◊: Q 8 6    ♣: J62

The bidding went, ONE CLUB on my left. PASS. ONE HEART on my right. PASS from me. TWO HEARTS on my left. PASS. PASS. Not vulnerable against vulnerable, I balanced with a bold TWO SPADES. After a little bit of thought my left hand opponent bid THREE HEARTS. Great! I had accomplished my mission! What I hadn't noticed, however, was the way David's eyes lit up after my bid.

With only a slight hesitation, he bid THREE SPADES. Oh oh. What had I done? Waiting for a DOUBLE, I heard a hesitant PASS on my right. I passed and left hand opponent went into the tank. Please God, don't let him double. Amazingly, he came out with FOUR HEARTS. Thank you, God, thank you. But wait. David had a driven look in his eyes. Nothing was going to stop him now. I had created a monster. FOUR SPADES, he said with an almost religious fervor. The man on my right looked with befuddlement at his cards. I closed my eyes and waited for the double. But no. Incredibly, out came FIVE HEARTS.

They went down two, and a heated argument ensued.

"How could you go to five hearts after I only bid two?"

"You're the one who went to three and four. How could you do that?"

"I thought they could make three spades."

As we walked away from the table, I tried to tell David what I had been doing.

"I was only balancing," I said.

"Balancing?"

I started to explain.

"Well," he said, "isn't that what I did? I got them to five hearts, didn't I?"

♠ ♡ ◇ ♣

# C H A P T E R   4
# Doin' The Boards

*How many things would have appeared
incontestable in theory if genius had not
proved them wrong in practice?*
- Gotthold Ephraim Lessing

Ever since my wife Claudia and I, along with our friends David and Mary, got hooked on duplicate bridge, we have been striving to improve our respective games. We bought bridge books, read the daily Sheinwold column and played together on many a Saturday evening dealing out hands and discussing our bids and plays. Each of us would critique the other, but we all had the vague feeling that none of us really knew what we were talking about.

Then Claudia and I attended our first North American Bridge Championships in Toronto, and all of this changed for we discovered a great new study aide. Every novice game offered a hand record with analyses by experts. We brought home analysis sheets from every game we played there, and did so with every regional or national tournament that we attended since then. We dealt out the hands with David and Mary and then read the analyses aloud to see how we had done. Eventually, David bought a set of duplicate boards. One of us would make the boards ahead of time, and then the four of us would spend Saturday evening "doin' the boards," laying out the hands afterwards, and reading the analyses.

In those early days of bridge, our results were often vastly different from those suggested on the hand records. "All roads lead to 3NT," the analysis would say while we had wallowed in THREE CLUBS.

Gradually, however, our bidding and play began to resemble what the experts said was supposed to have happened.

Whenever we did the boards, I was the designated reader, and I grew somewhat fond of pointing out other people's errors–especially Claudia's. "You can't overcall with that kind of broken suit," I'd tell her, expecting the expert to agree. Much to my chagrin and the amusement of everyone else, however, the analysis that I would then read aloud would suggest doing exactly what Claudia had done.

The ultimate embarrassment came one night on board 13. As North, my hand was: ♠: K 8 5 ♡: A 3 2 ◊: Q 6 4 ♣: K Q 10 8. I opened ONE CLUB. Claudia bid ONE HEART, and I bid ONE NO TRUMP. Claudia perused her hand for a moment and then passed. I made two. The analysis complimented South if she passed ONE NO TRUMP. It was true that she had five hearts, but otherwise her hand was flat. "South has no trump shape and only five hearts," said the analysis "making it unwise for South to rebid the five card suit."

"That's just what I thought," Claudia said.

"Of course," I muttered. "That's pretty obvious. Next board."

On board 14 I picked up: ♠: Q J 9 ♡: Q 9 8 5 4 ◊: K 7 3 ♣: J 9. Claudia opened ONE CLUB and I bid ONE HEART. When Claudia bid ONE NO TRUMP, I evaluated my holding. I reasoned that my hearts without any spots would be more valuable as trumps. TWO HEARTS, I bid. Alas, the K J 10 7 of trumps were on my left. I had to lose three hearts and three aces for down one. "Bad heart break," I mumbled and picked up the sheet to read the analysis. Board 14, however, did not look or sound anything like the one we had just played.

"You guys messed up when you made the boards," I told Dave and Mary. "This isn't the right board. We stared at the four hands:

```
              ♠ K 8 5
              ♡ A 3 2
              ◊ Q 6 4
              ♣ K Q 10 8

  ♠ 10 3 2          N          ♠ A 7 6 4
  ♡ K J 10 6                   ♡ 7
  ◊ A 10 5     W  ✦  E         ◊ J 9 8 2
  ♣ A 6 2                      ♣ 7 5 4 3
                    S
              ♠ Q J 9
              ♡ Q 9 8 5 4
              ◊ K 7 3
              ♣ J 9
```

Suddenly, it dawned on us. This wasn't board 14 at all but board 13 with the North-South hands switched. We had played the same board twice, each with our partner's hand, and no one had noticed. Claudia passed 1NT with the South hand, while I had bid TWO HEARTS with it. Claudia, Dave and Mary were laughing so hard, they were doubled over.

"With a better heart split, I would have made it," I tried to argue over their convulsions, but this only evoked more and even louder howls.

Personally, I didn't see what was so funny. Do you think they set me up?

♠ ♡ ◇ ♣

# CHAPTER 5
# In Pursuit Of The Elusive Cookie

*Fame is delightful, but as collateral it does not rank high.*
- Elbert Hubbard

It was the 1991 summer NABC (The North American Bridge Championships) in Boston. My wife Claudia and I had the time and the money for only two days of competition. One day we played in a Flight C pairs game. The only memorable thing about it was a hand against two Oriental students from MIT. Claudia opened ONE NO TRUMP. I had the four kings, a flat hand, and nothing else, so I raised her to THREE NO TRUMP. She made four, and after the play was over, she commented that she hated to open ONE NO TRUMP with just the four aces and nothing else.

"I didn't have anything but the four kings," I said.

"Wait," said one of the students, looking at his hand. "I had the four queens."

"I had the four jacks!" said the other student.

By the way, one of the students ducked his queen at a key moment in the hand, which held Claudia to four. The two students, we later learned, went on to win the event.

On our second day at the tournament, we played in a 0-200 Swiss with some friends. In our first round, we blitzed a team from Montreal, and for the rest of the day we were in and out of first place. Pretty heady stuff for four novices from New Hampshire.

After dinner, we went up to our friends' hotel room to relax before the evening session. On the way back down in a crowded elevator, a garrulous bellhop asked what we were all doing at the hotel. "Playing bridge," we intoned. "How are you all doing?" he asked. There was an assortment of mutters and moans ranging from a few "goods" to quite a few "not so goods."

"What do you all get for winning?" the bellhop asked.

"Masterpoints," someone said.

"What do you do with those?"

"Nothing."

"Then what are you all doing here spending all of this money?"

No answer. On the way out of the elevator, I recognized a tall, curly-haired man near the back. I nudged my wife and pointed out Eddie Kantar.

"Who?"

"Eddie Kantar. The bridge champion and the writer."

"Oh."

"I just bought his book. I could have had him autograph it, but I left it in the room."

Before the second session, we were to hear the Granovetters speak on the topic of "Husband and Wife." Claudia and I had already suffered through some of the pitfalls of playing with a spouse, and we had chosen this specific day at the NABC because of the scheduled talk.

To our dismay, the Granovetters canceled because Matt was playing in the Spingold. "What's that?" my wife asked. "I'm not sure," I said. "Some national level team game, I think."

Alan Truscott gave a talk about when to go up with the queen when you have Qx in dummy after a lead in that suit against your notrump contract. The situation came up for me about a year later, but I had completely forgotten what Truscott said, and I got it wrong.

Before the second session started, I had to go to the men's room. My teammate warned me of the crowded men's rooms in the hotel and directed me to a little-used facility by one of the back elevators. Sure enough, I was alone in the rest room until a tall, curly haired man walked in. *It was Eddie Kantar.* Should I say something to him? No, it would sound stupid. But I really wanted an autograph, and I didn't care if it did sound stupid.

"I can't believe it," I blurted. "I just bought your book this afternoon, and I'd really like to have it autographed. I've seen you twice, but both times I haven't had my book with me."

"Well," said Kantar with a somewhat wary expression as though he thought he should get out of that bathroom, "don't worry. I'll be around."

Back in the tournament, I pulled out these cards on the 56th deal of the day:

♠: K J 9 6 2 ♡: K Q 8 5 ◇: Q 7 4 ♣: 5. There were three passes to me. Eleven high-card points, and I didn't have two quick tricks. I passed, and it cost us the event. Our opponents opened ONE SPADE and rebid TWO HEARTS over the ONE NO TRUMP response. Making two. We lost the match by two imps and the event by two Victory Points. The shiny first place trophies went to another team, and we got the second place prize: four packages of Pepperidge Farm Chocolate Chip Cookies. The third place team mumbled that, unlike the first two teams, they had won all of their matches and still finished third.

Amidst the commiserations and congratulations, I saw Kantar standing by himself on the other side of the lobby. And I had my book with me! I approached him again. His expression said that he had probably better give this little man who had been trailing him all day an autograph or he would most likely follow him home on the plane.

"How did you do in the Spingold?" I asked him.

"If I tell you," he said, "you probably wouldn't want this autograph."

All in all, a pretty successful day. Second place, 3.26 masterpoints, and of course, our cookies, a strange but tasty prize. Back home in New Hampshire, I tried to tell my non-bridge playing son Phil about our day's adventure. In his inimitable way, he managed to put everything into perspective.

"Wow," he said, munching on one of the Pepperidge Farm Chocolate Chips, "you got Eddie Kantar's autograph?"

"Yep."

"And he's a world champion bridge player?"

"Yep."

"Gosh. He must have lots of cookies."

♠ ♡ ◇ ♣

# C H A P T E R  6
# Think

*Whenever I think, I make a mistake.*
- Roger Stevens

"Think!" I can still hear Frank, our first bridge teacher, exhorting us to use just a little bit of logic, just a smidgen of reasoning at the bridge table.

My wife Claudia and I, intrigued with the game of duplicate bridge, had been advised by our friends from Vermont to take lessons as they had done. I called our local adult education office, and they said they had never offered bridge lessons but that it sounded like a good idea, and they would ask around to see if anyone was interested in teaching it. Did I have any ideas? I gave them the names of some of the players from the local club where we had begun to play, and a week later they called me and said that one of the players, Frank, had offered to teach. Classes would begin in six weeks.

Frank was not one to spend much time at the blackboard. He liked to play the game, and he thought that we would too. As soon as possible, we set up tables in the classroom and took our first shots at bidding, declarer play and defense.

All the while, Frank would wander from table to table, looking over our shoulders and imploring us to "Think!"

I was West:

| West | North | East | South |
|------|-------|------|-------|
|      |       |      | 1 ♡   |
| Pass | 1 NT  | Pass | 2 ◊   |
| All Pass |   |      |       |

My hand was: ♠: Q 6 ♡: A J 8 7 ◊: 10 7 3 ♣: Q 8 7 4. On lead, I reached for a club.

"Think!" Frank said.

I cringed. I didn't know Frank was standing behind me, and I thought I had been thinking. Wasn't fourth best a good lead?

Well, maybe a spade was best in hopes of getting a ruff. I fingered the queen of spades.

"Come on, Carl. You're not thinking."

A heart? That couldn't be right, could it?

"Can't you visualize South ruffing his hearts in dummy?" Frank asked. "When the opponents avoid no trump, lead a trump. And when you get in with the ace of hearts, lead another trump. Think!"

I can sometimes still hear Frank when I'm at the table. In fact, I heard him loud and clear on this deal:

```
                    ♠ A
                    ♡ A 10 2
                    ◊ A J 8 6 2
                    ♣ 10 6 4 2

      ♠ 8               N              ♠ J 6 4 2
      ♡ J 9 8 4                        ♡ K 7 6 5
      ◊ Q 10 9 7 4   W  +  E           ◊ K 5
      ♣ Q J 7                          ♣ K 9 8
                        S
                    ♠ K Q 10 9 7 5 3
                    ♡ Q 3
                    ◊ 3
                    ♣ A 5 3
```

22

I was South in 4 SPADES, and I got a diamond lead. What could go wrong? I won the ace of diamonds, and at trick two played dummy's ace of spades. Down one!

There were four spades to the jack on my right–and I can guard against the bad trump split by ruffing a diamond at trick two. Next I play a spade to dummy's ace and ruff another diamond.

When I cash the king of spades and get the bad news, I can cash the club ace, lead a heart to dummy's ace and ruff another diamond. I am left with ♠: Q 10 ♡:Q D:— ♣: 5 3. The opponents can cash a heart and two clubs, but they can't prevent me from scoring both spades and my game.

I got an above average board for down one–most pairs were in 3NT going down two. That's small consolation, however, when you get a good result but didn't play good bridge.

I know, Frank, I know. Think!

♠ ♡ ◇ ♣

C H A P T E R   7
# Bridge Is For The Bold

*A teacher affects eternity; he can never tell*
*where his influence stops.*
-Henry Adams

Frank, our first bridge teacher, was fond of the saying, "Bridge is for the bold." When Claudia and I started playing against Frank in the area's duplicate clubs, we found out what he meant.

Frank was fond of shooting from the hip. He took wild chances in the balancing seat, and he led doubletons and an occasional singleton against notrump contracts, causing many a declarer to misplace the outstanding cards and misplay the hand.

He opened light and bid games so thin that you would have to go to the next deal to find the game-going trick. Still, he managed to bring home many of these contracts, and we thought he was a magician able to pull tricks out of his sleeve.

To Frank, this was all part of the game's fun. Bridge and poker were not that dissimilar. You had to be bold. Of course, that boldness often got Frank into desperate situations, but that was okay with him. Desperate times called for desperate measures. Your play just had to be up to your boldness. And you had to keep a straight face. Don't let the opponents know you're in trouble.

I didn't live up to Frank's advice at a recent sectional Swiss Teams. I was South.

♠ J 8 5
♡ 3
◊ A Q 8 7 4
♣ A K 8 4

♠ A K 9 6
♡ A 6 5 4
◊ K 3
♣ Q 10 5

Partner and I had a bidding accident. He was afraid of the singleton heart and tried to keep me out of 3NT, but instead we got to 4NT. The opening lead was the king of hearts. Oops. I ran three diamond tricks, and East discarded on the third one. Now I led a club from dummy. I knew East was likely to have long clubs, and I should finesse the 10, but I was scared of losing unnecessarily to the jack. I cashed the queen, king and ace. Sure enough, West discarded on the third club.

In desperation, I played the ace and king of spades, but the queen didn't drop. Down one. At the other table, 3NT made three, and we lost the match. Why hadn't I been bold enough to finesse that club?

Claudia, on the other hand, remembered Frank's lesson in a later match.

**DLR: South   VUL: N-S**

```
                    ♠ 10 7 6 5 4
                    ♡ A 9
                    ◇ J 5 4
                    ♣ 7 5 3

   ♠ A J 2              N              ♠ Q 8
   ♡ K 5 4                             ♡ 8 7 6 3 2
   ◇ 10 8 3       W  ✦  E              ◇ K 6 2
   ♣ 10 8 6 2                          ♣ K 9 4
                       S
                    ♠ K 9 3
                    ♡ Q J 10
                    ◇ A Q 9 7
                    ♣ A Q J
```

With her 19 high-card points, Claudia decided to open 2NT. Too many times with hands like this, she opened ONE DIAMOND and had to play it there when notrump was the best contract. I transferred her to spades and bid game. The opening lead was a club. That was one hurdle.

She had only one entry to dummy for a diamond finesse, but how would she avoid three spade losers? This was a stratified Swiss, and at the time we were Flight C players. This match was against a Flight A team, so maybe these A players would fall for a bit of subterfuge. Boldly she led the king of spades making everyone except East think that she also had the queen, but East did not matter. West took her ace and led another club. Claudia won this and led the three of spades from her hand. West stared long and hard at dummy's ten of spades and, swindled, played her jack only to see her partner's queen crash on the same trick.

At the other table, the contract was ONE DIAMOND. Claudia feared this would happen, so she had boldly opened 2NT. Her declarer play was up to her boldness, and the vulnerable game won us the match. At least one of us had been paying attention in Frank's bridge class.

♠ ♡ ◇ ♣

# C H A P T E R   8
# The Virtue Of Silence

*That man's silence is wonderful to listen to.*
- Thomas Hardy

I admit it. I've become a bidding fool, addicted to the premise that bridge is a bidder's game. If there were such a thing as Bidder's Anonymous, my partners would make sure that I did not miss a single monthly meeting. But hey, I paid my entry fee, so I have a right to bid whenever I want to, don't I?

Unfortunately for my partners, the first lesson that ever sunk in with me about one of the nuances of the game of bridge- not the basics but the nuances- was that it was not right to let your opponents settle comfortably at the two level. You had to bid. If, for instance, you hold:

♠: K J 8 7  ♡:J 4 3  ◇: Q 8 7 5  ♣: Q 3 and the bidding goes:

|  | **Partner** | **You** |  |
|------|---------|------|------|
| 1 ♣ | Pass | 1 ♡ | Pass |
| 2 ♡ | Pass | Pass | ? |

You should bid. This is called a balancing bid. Your poor partner could not conveniently enter the auction himself, so you have to bid for him–either double or bid TWO SPADES.

Oscar, the first life master I ever played with, taught me this lesson. Push! Do your opponents look content? That's not good. Push them higher. Provoke their discontent. Of course, you might go for that occasional prodigious penalty, but that doesn't matter. The successful duplicate player is not one who sits back and lets his opponents have their way with him. If pushing gets you a good result 51% of the time, then push you should.

This was right up my alley. I loved to bid, and Oscar was giving me his blessing to do so. Observe this example from a world wide instant matchpoint game that I played in many years after Oscar had taught me his philosophy. At favorable vulnerability I held: ♠: 8 ♡: A J 8 4 2 ◊: A Q J 3 ♣: J 9 6 and opened ONE HEART. My left-hand opponent overcalled ONE SPADE, partner bid TWO HEARTS, and right-hand opponent jumped to FOUR SPADES. There you are. Any thoughts? Do the opponents sound content? Oscar would not have hesitated, and neither did I- I bid FIVE HEARTS. Left hand opponent, looking perplexed, was obviously not expecting this. After some long thought, he unhappily bid FIVE SPADES, and all passed. This was the full deal:

**DLR: SOUTH    VUL: E-W**

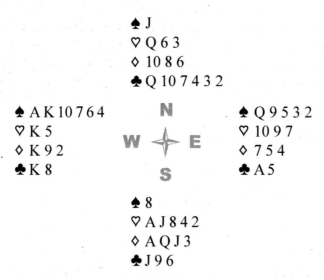

FIVE SPADES down one gave us 93 out of 100 worldwide matchpoints. If West had doubled FIVE HEARTS, we would have gotten 84 out of 100 points. Thanks, Oscar.

But wait. Oscar wasn't finished with me yet. He taught me another way to push, with the preempt. You mean I can bid when I really don't have a bid? Oh boy. Watch out! My weak three bids became paltry, and some of my weak two bids bordered on the downright criminal. Once, I opened TWO SPADES with : S: Q107532 H: 874 D: 87 C: 53. Unfortunately, for all of my future partners, I got a great result. There was no stopping me now.

I convinced my partners to play weak jump shifts as responders. "How often do you have a huge hand?" I asked. "Most of the time you have nothing. Now you can bid with nothing. Isn't that great?"

"Wait a minute," Oscar said when he saw the crazed look in my eyes and realized that he had created a monster, "there's another word in bridge that you need to learn: PASS"

"But you said..."

"Never mind what I said. There is a time for everything," he intoned biblically, "and sometimes it is better just to pass."

And thus it came to pass that I learned the virtue of silence in bridge. One of David Byrd's most amusing characters in his "Bridge With the Abbot" series is a monk who has taken the vow of silence. This monk is dealt wildly distributional hands, but because of his vow, he never bids. Many of my partners say I should take this vow too! Observe this deal from a board-a-match game which we played against a top New England expert:

**DLR: SOUTH     VUL: NONE**

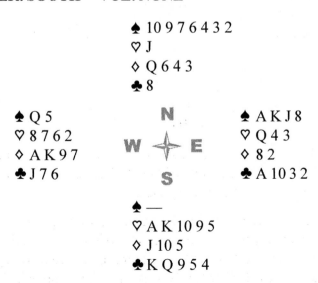

```
                    ♠ 10 9 7 6 4 3 2
                    ♡ J
                    ◊ Q 6 4 3
                    ♣ 8
   ♠ Q 5                              ♠ A K J 8
   ♡ 8 7 6 2          N               ♡ Q 4 3
   ◊ A K 9 7      W  ✧  E             ◊ 8 2
   ♣ J 7 6            S               ♣ A 10 3 2
                    ♠ —
                    ♡ A K 10 9 5
                    ◊ J 10 5
                    ♣ K Q 9 5 4
```

Sitting South, I opened ONE HEART. West passed as did my partner. Yes, we were playing weak jump shifts and yes, he had all those spades, but he passed.

The expert, sitting East, doubled for take-out, and I then came in with TWO CLUBS. West passed, and partner passed again! Now came the reward. The expert, East, bid TWO SPADES, and everyone passed. We took six tricks and declarer was down one.

"You passed?" I asked partner.

He nodded yes.

"With all those spades?"

Again he nodded yes.

"When we play weak jump shifts?"

Another nod.

"I never would have passed that hand in a million years," I declared.

"I know," partner said, and then he quoted Oscar, "sometimes it's better just to pass."

I had to agree.

At the other table, the contract was also TWO SPADES- by North-South! Down two. A fun board for us to win, and an invaluable lesson for me. Oscar was right–Ssshhh!

♠ ♡ ◇ ♣

## C H A P T E R  9
# Necessity

*Necessity is the mother of invention*
*-Anonymous Latin saying*

Unfortunately, for most of us, the way we learn things in bridge is the hard way. We err, and then we realize what we should have done. After we make the same mistake enough times, the lesson finally sinks in.

I wonder if the inventors of various plays in bridge didn't stumble upon them in just this manner. First they made a mistake, then they observed their poor result, and only then did they think of a way around that poor result. Can you imagine, for example, the first person to ever pull off a squeeze play? He was most certainly, like me, a chronic overbidder who found himself going down in game after overbid game. Then, one time, when he realized that he was once again one trick short of his contract, and he was once again going to have to face the wrath of his partner, he delayed the inevitable by playing out all of his trumps and, voila, like magic his game-going trick appeared.

It must have been the same with the first ever unblocking play. I'll never forget my initial unblocking play–or at least the necessity for it. As you will see, recognizing the necessity for that play and actually making it were only wistful afterthoughts.

My wife Claudia and I were playing in our very first sectional tournament. Incredibly, for us, we would have finished second in our flight had I recognized the opportunity to make my first ever unblocking play. Here was the fateful hand:

**DLR: WEST  VUL: N-S**

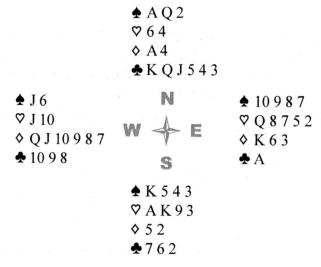

```
                    ♠ A Q 2
                    ♡ 6 4
                    ◊ A 4
                    ♣ K Q J 5 4 3

      ♠ J 6              N            ♠ 10 9 8 7
      ♡ J 10                          ♡ Q 8 7 5 2
      ◊ Q J 10 9 8 7  W  ✦  E         ◊ K 6 3
      ♣ 10 9 8            S           ♣ A

                    ♠ K 5 4 3
                    ♡ A K 9 3
                    ◊ 5 2
                    ♣ 7 6 2
```

North-South bid to THREE NO TRUMP after Claudia, who was sitting West, had opened a weak TWO DIAMONDS. North overcalled THREE CLUBS, and I bid THREE DIAMONDS. South, looking at stoppers in both majors, gambled that his partner had a diamond stopper for his vulnerable overcall and bid THREE NO TRUMP.

Claudia led the queen of diamonds. Declarer ducked the ace, and here was my first chance to unblock the suit and play my king. But why would I overtake my wife's winner with my own? I played my highest diamond, the beginning of a clever echo. I had read about echoes and knew that they showed a strong interest in the suit that was led. Claudia continued with the jack of diamonds, and declarer, perforce, took his ace.

Here it was. My last chance to be a hero. But why would I even think of needlessly throwing my king under declarer's ace? Silly notion. I completed my echo with the three of diamonds, and declarer now knocked out my ace of clubs.

Smugly I played my winning king of diamonds, and that was when it hit me. Declarer showed out of diamonds, and I stared across the table at Claudia who held all of those good diamonds, those good but absolutely unreachable diamonds. The abyss between her hand and mine might as well have been the Grand Canyon. How could I reach those diamonds? Claudia gave me one of her patented "nice going bozo" looks. Vainly I tried a heart, but declarer had the rest of the tricks and an absolute top.

Other pairs were in a club partial or FIVE CLUBS, the only safe game contract unless West doesn't open TWO DIAMONDS. But Claudia had opened that weak two bid indicating the path to the defeat of this contract if only I had unblocked the suit. We had been given a chance for our own top and second place in our first sectional tournament, but allowing the opponents to take ten tricks in NO TRUMP plummeted us to the ignominy of sixth place.

Why didn't you throw your king under the ace?" Claudia asked me. Isn't that what they call an unblocking play? Didn't you see that somewhere in all those bridge books that you read?"

"I know what an unblocking play is," I said defensively. "I just grabbed the wrong card."

The first person to ever conceive of an unblocking play must have figured it out when he found himself in a position just like mine, cashed his winner, and then realized he could not reach his partner.

Later that night, in a fitful sleep, I dreamed I was defending the very same hand except that, in a bizarre twist, Greg, my boss at work, was kibitzing me. I made the exact same play, grimly holding on to my winning king.

"Why didn't you throw the king under the ace?" Greg asked me after the hand was over. "Then you could have reached your partner with the third diamond."

"But Greg," I said, "you don't even play bridge."

"True," he conceded, "but that's a simple unblocking play. Everybody knows that!"

# C H A P T E R   1 0
# Eine Kleine Bridge Talk

*So this is what our lives have been given to find,*
*A language that can serve our purposes.*
- Hugh McDiarmid

C an you imagine someone who has never played bridge listening to a "pack" of bridge players indulging in a little bridge talk? It must sound like a foreign language to them: ruffs, trumps, splinters (ouch!), slams, namyats (huh?), doubles, discards, come-ons, strip and endplays, and revokes.

"What in the world are you people talking about?" I've been asked on numerous occasions.

Eric, my brother-in-law, loves to talk bridge. Whenever he stops in at our house and my son sees the two of us together, he begins a count-down: "five, four, three, two, one...BRIDGE TALK!" When our two families go out to eat, Eric and I are not allowed to sit anywhere near one another. "No BRIDGE TALK," we are warned by both of our spouses.

David and Mary, colleagues at the high school where I teach, are also fellow bridge players. When the three of us first got into duplicate bridge, our favorite lunchtime activity was A LITTLE BRIDGE TALK. We would ask for the traveling scoreslips from the previous week's duplicate game and bring them to lunch with us, where the three of us would pore over them like scholars over the Dead Sea Scrolls trying to detect what we had done right or wrong on each board.

By the way, this is a great way for you and your partner to review your actions from your latest game and learn from your mistakes. There is always something to be gleaned from the scoreslips. For instance:

| N-S PAIR NO. | CONTRACT | BY | MADE | DOWN | SCORE | | E-W PAIR NO. | MATCH POINTS |
|---|---|---|---|---|---|---|---|---|
| | | | | | N-S | E-W | | |
| 1 | 4 H | N | 4 | | 420 | | 1 | 5 |
| 7 | 4 S | E | 4 | | | 420 | 6 | 0 |
| 6 | 5 H | N | | 1 | | 50 | 4 | 1 |
| 5 | 5 SX | E | | 1 | 100 | | 2 | 3 |
| 4 | 5 S | E | | 1 | 50 | | 7 | 2 |
| 3 | 5 HX | N | 5 | | 710 | | 5 | 6 |
| 2 | 3 H | N | 5 | | 200 | | 3 | 4 |

"I've read this somewhere," I said. "The side that quits first in a high competitive auction usually gets the worst result. We let them play FOUR SPADES and got a zero."

"They bid five spades against us," David said, "and the best that we could do is double. Pair 2 got a better score than we did, and they didn't even bid game."

Then:

| N-S PAIR NO. | CONTRACT | BY | MADE | DOWN | SCORE | | E-W PAIR NO. | MATCH POINTS |
|---|---|---|---|---|---|---|---|---|
| | | | | | N-S | E-W | | |
| 1 | 3 NT | E | | 1 | 100 | | 4 | 4 1/2 |
| 2 | 3 NT | W | 3 | | | 600 | 5 | 1/2 |
| 3 | 3 NT | E | | 1 | 100 | | 6 | 4 1/2 |
| 4 | 3 NT | E | 3 | | | 600 | 3 | 1/2 |
| 5 | 3 NT | E | | 1 | 100 | | 1 | 4 1/2 |
| 6 | 3 NT | E | | 1 | 100 | | 2 | 4 1/2 |
| 7 | 3 D | W | 3 | | | 110 | 7 | 2 |

"They made 3NT against us and against you too," Mary said. How were all those people setting it."

We got a piece of paper from the copier and reconstructed the hand:

**DLR SOUTH VUL: E-W**

```
                    ♠ J 7
                    ♡ 10 5 4 3
                    ◇ Q J 6 4
                    ♣ J 7 4
  ♠ A 3                 N              ♠ K 8 6 5
  ♡ A J 8 7                            ♡ Q 9 6
  ◇ A 9 5        W  ⬦  E              ◇ K 8 7 2
  ♣ 9 8 6 2              S             ♣ A Q
                    ♠ Q 10 9 4 2
                    ♡ K 2
                    ◇ 10 3
                    ♣ K 10 5 3
```

"West was declarer," Mary said. "They bid diamonds, so I led a heart. West won the king with his ace and finessed with the nine of hearts at trick two. That gave him four heart tricks plus two each in spades and diamonds and one in clubs. How come you didn't set it? You were on lead, weren't you?"

"They bid spades on my right," I admitted, "so I led a club right into the ace-queen."

On went our bridge talk through the lunch period as we discussed one board after another, our talk peppered with the colorful language of bridge- contracts, leads, fixes, tops and bottoms. Whenever the three of us started talking bridge, the rest of our table in the lunchroom would inevitably get up and leave.

"There they go again," said a French teacher at our table gathering his belongings and heading off in search of a conversation he could understand. "What on earth are they talking about?"

"I have no clue," said a disgruntled Spanish teacher who got up to leave as well. "All I know is that somebody always has a stiff king. I have no idea what that is, but somebody always has one."

Don't you just love bridge talk!

♠ ♡ ◇ ♣

PART TWO
# The People

One of the most entertaining aspects of playing duplicate bridge is the unique cast of characters that my wife and I have encountered in our travels through bridge country. We have two memories of our first experience with duplicate in a little eight-table game: the preposterous yet absolute panic we felt, and the motley crew of individuals that lay in wait for us at those tables. This was indeed a curious group of people.

Imagine this at the very first table. We were terrified enough to begin with, but sitting North was an older gentleman with a bottle of beer on the table in front of him and a cigarette clenched between his teeth (club rules were somewhat looser 20 years ago). His name was Tom, and he was declarer for the first board. When he drew trumps against us, it was with such a ferocity that we thought he was going to hit us with the cards. He pulled the ace of trumps from his hand and slapped it on the table using his whole upper body in the motion like a pitcher firing a fast ball. THWACK! Then the king of trumps. THWACK! Thankful that the trumps had split and we both could follow suit, we sheepishly tabled our losers. In the years since that night, Tom, a kindly and intelligent man, has become a good friend, but we will never forget our first experience at his table.

Next was Oscar, another of the many experienced players in that session against whom we felt several levels less than competent. Although I never would have thought it at the time, Oscar would later become one of my regular partners. On that night, though, he was just another intimidating, larger than life player. Oscar's shtick was his painfully slow yet

37

theatrical play of the cards. When it was his turn to play, he studied his hand carefully, searching, searching for just the right card. After what seemed like an eternity, he selected a card, extracted it from his hand with thumb and trigger finger, stood it on the table before him, then held it, held it, held it until, finally, like the blade on a guillotine, he let it drop, exposed at last for all to see.

Then there was Jack- hard of hearing and just a little bit confused. Jack had not drawn all of the trumps in one deal. He then led a suit in which I was void, so I ruffed Jack's card. He paid me no attention whatsoever and led his next card.

"He trumped it, Jack," his partner called loudly to him across the table.

"Huh?" Jack said as he flashed me an irritated glare then played his next card anyway.

"No, Jack," his partner called, louder this time, "he trumped it."

"Huh?" Jack grunted, again flashing me the look, and again playing his next card.

Jack's partner had to pick up the card from the table himself and put it back in Jack's hand. "You can't play Jack. HE TRUMPED IT."

Another daunting pair was Ed and Frank who played the Woodson Two-Way No-Trump.

"ONE NO TRUMP," said Frank back in those days before bidding boxes.

"Alert," said Ed.

"Yes?" I inquired.

"Could be strong, could be weak."

"Excuse me?"

"Could be 10 to 12, or could be 16 to 18."

"Well which is it?"

"I'll ask him on my next bid."

How were a couple of novices supposed to deal with that? Not very well, I'll tell you.

When we eventually ventured beyond the club level and began to play in tournaments, we found that sectionals, regionals and nationals were also peopled with their fair share of eccentrics and originals.

There was the man we called Karl Marx- he really did look like Marx, dressed in black and punctuated with a wild head and face full of unruly black hair. I don't recall his real name, but everyone in our neck of Bridge Country knew whom you meant when you said you had played Karl Marx. Karl had a reputation of always bidding 3NT at his first opportunity when the hand belonged to his side. The field would be in three of a minor or four of a major, but Karl would be in THREE NO TRUMP, usually making for a top board.

Then there was FIDEL CASTRO who inevitably showed up on Swiss Team Sunday with his band of followers. Fidel always wore the same outfit, a beret and military fatigues to complement his full beard and complete the authentic Fidel look. Between rounds, Fidel could always be seen standing at his team's table and wildly lecturing them about one of the hands they had just played.

And there was Bat Masterson, replete with fancy suit, spats, and a diamond-studded cane. And how about the Swami, arrayed in full Indian robes, turban and a jewel on his forehead? One time the Swami stopped about five cards into the play of a hand which he was declaring, put his head on the table and went into an apparent trance. Several minutes later he rose, smiling, laid his cards out on the table and claimed.

You get the idea. Part of the fun of this funny game is the wild pack of players you'll meet when you play it.

Here are five stories about some of my favorites.

♠ ♡ ◇ ♣

# C H A P T E R  1 1
# Captain Bic and The Lessons of Bridge and Life

*Draw from others the lesson that may profit yourself.*
- Terrence  (190-159 BC.)

Since we began playing bridge, my wife Claudia and I have met a myriad of characters who taught us much about bridge and about life. Perhaps the most unique of all these people was a dapper gentleman who will everlastingly live on in our minds as Captain Bic.

We met Captain Bic at a regional tournament in Cromwell, Connecticut. It was almost game time when Claudia and I arrived at our assigned table against one wall of the crowded hotel ballroom for the afternoon stratified pairs. An older gentleman and his wife were already sitting North-South. I noticed their entry lying on the table and was relieved to see we would be starting off against another flight C pair. The lady sat patiently waiting for the game to begin, but the gentleman was a veritable flurry of activity. He had one briefcase open on the table and another on the floor. Papers were spread out everywhere. With his snow-white hair and mustache, his sport coat and ascot, he cut quite a dashing figure. Most prominent about him, however, was a plastic pen holder in his vest pocket with three tiers of assorted pens and pencils. There must have been more than 20 writing implements jammed into that holder. Thus, Captain Bic!

The two of them greeted us quite amicably, but then Captain Bic went about his business writing on, shuffling and sorting his papers. I asked him what he was doing, and he said he was running a couple of businesses- a consulting firm and an engineering firm. Duly impressed, I sat down to fill out our entry.

"I'm sorry," I said. "I forgot a pencil. Could a borrow one to do the entry?"

"Sure," said the Captain, "I've got one here somewhere. Let me see."

And he went about bumbling through both of his briefcases in search of a pencil, totally ignoring the triple-tiered pen and pencil holder in his pocket!

When the game began, I took out this hand against Captain Bic and his wife:

♠: Q J 9 8 7 ♡: A 4 ◊: A Q 7 3 ♣: 10 8 In first position, I opened ONE SPADE. Claudia responded TWO DIAMONDS. I raised to THREE DIAMONDS, and she bid FOUR SPADES. Captain Bic led the king of clubs, and these were our two hands:

```
        ♠ A K 10
        ♡ 8 5 3
        ◊ K J 6 2
        ♣ J 9 3

              N

       W  ✦  E

              S

        ♠ Q J 9 8 7
        ♡ A 4
        ◊ A Q 7 3
        ♣ 10 8
```

I counted my tricks. The first board of the day was going to be flat. The opponents could take their two club tricks and a heart, but nothing more. Mrs. Bic played high-low to the first two clubs and followed with the queen on the third one. I ruffed the third club and led a spade. Captain Bic pitched a diamond! I now had to lose a spade along with the other three losers.

"Bad trump break," sympathized Mrs. Bic.

After dinner, I went back into the ballroom to check our posted scores. Captain Bic was there writing down his scores. "How did you do?" I asked.

"Not grandly," he said, smiling as if it didn't much matter. "How about yourself?"

"I don't think we did very well either."

"You have to remember something," Captain Bic said. "Our patience will achieve more than our force. That goes for bridge and for life. Take board one against us today, for example. You were cold for FOUR SPADES."

"How do you figure that?"

"How many tricks could you count?"

"Ten."

"Was there any play for an eleventh?" he asked.

"I don't think so. No."

"Then why were you in such a rush to take your tricks? You young people. Always in a rush. Throw your losing heart on the third club. Win any return including a club which you can now trump on the board, and take your ten tricks. Patience is always rewarded."

I had read about such loser on loser plays, but I had blown the opportunity to make one at the table.

"Don't look so glum," said Captain Bic. "Look, you still wound up with an average on the board. Some Souths went down one, some were doubled, and, of course, there were some who made the contract. See? Not so bad huh? And look at this. You finished tied for fourth-fifth in your section. Point four-five master points."

"Point four-five. Wow!"

"Things are never as bad as they seem," he said. "And even if they are, there will always be other days. One more thing you should remember. In life, bridge doesn't mean a blessed thing. Don't be so serious."

And with that, Captain Bic headed madly off in all directions.

♠ ♡ ◇ ♣

# CHAPTER 12
# Playing For Average With Jim

*An expert is someone who knows some of the worst mistakes that can be made in his subject and who manages to avoid them.*
- Werner Heisenberg

"Don't do anything crazy," I told my wife Claudia. "Just play for average. All we need are two average boards and we'll win."

It was Sunday afternoon at the club, and Claudia and I were having a really good game. You remember how that feels, don't you? People welcome you to their table and then do everything they can possibly think of to give you good boards. The tops fall from the sky like manna. The good news was we only had one round to go. The bad news was we had to play Jim, the local expert.

Every bridge club has a player like Jim, I'm sure. The player who always seems to win or come close to it week after week and who always manages to somehow, some way finagle three good boards out of you and your partner.

In the few years that Claudia and I had been playing duplicate, we had seen Jim do squeezes (easy!), endplays, eliminations, trump coups, smother plays, and trump reduction plays. Inevitably, the opportunity for one of these esoteric plays would present itself during our round with Jim, and we would walk away from his table the proud possessors of three lousy boards. And we always knew, just knew, that if Jim eschewed THREE NO TRUMP he would be on his way to a cold minor suit slam that no one else in the room would even consider.

Average, just average. That was the best you could hope for with Jim. And that was all we needed Sunday afternoon. Three average boards.

43

My only hope was that Claudia wouldn't be intimidated by Jim and give away our good game.

I, however, was the nervous one and promptly took the first hand out of the board and dropped all of the cards on the floor. After a sheepish apology, and after I had gotten my hand back together, I looked at these cards: ♠: K 9 6 ♡: J 8 5 2 ◇: Q 4 ♣: 9 7 5. In first position with favorable vulnerability, what would you have said? I hope it's not PASS, because that's what I said. Look closely. There are only 12 cards here.

Jim and his partner bid unopposed to THREE NO TRUMP. During the play, I won my king of spades. I later pitched a club on the fourth round of spades. With four tricks left to play, I suddenly noticed that I had only three cards left. We looked around, and there on the floor on the far side of Jim's foot was my fourth spade. I had revoked.

All around the room, the board was absolutely flat- THREE NO TRUMP, making three. Due to the revoke, however, Jim was awarded an extra trick. A cold top for him and a resounding bottom for us. Claudia gave me one of her inimitable "nice going" looks. I couldn't believe it. With expiation on my mind, I picked up the next hand. I had to get us back to average: ♠: 10 7 3 ♡: A K ◇: A K J 10 9 7 4 ♣: K

I counted the cards three times. Yes, there were thirteen cards. In second position I opened ONE DIAMOND. DOUBLE from Jim's partner on my left. Claudia passed and Jim bid ONE HEART. I jumped to THREE DIAMONDS. Jim's partner bid THREE HEARTS followed by two passes. What would you have done? I decided to push. FOUR DIAMONDS, I said. Jim's partner took the bait and bid FOUR HEARTS.

I had done it! If anyone could evaluate a hand, it was Jim. He had passed THREE HEARTS even after his partner's strong bidding. I figured I would get one or two diamonds and two hearts. Besides, my partner had to have something over there, because Jim didn't figure to have much at all. I doubled FOUR HEARTS and led my ace of diamonds. Jim had a scowl on his face, but alas, this was the full deal:

**DLR: SOUTH    VUL: BOTH**

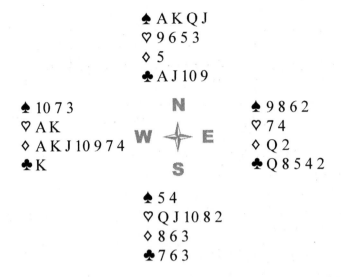

```
                    ♠ A K Q J
                    ♡ 9 6 5 3
                    ◊ 5
                    ♣ A J 10 9

    ♠ 10 7 3              N              ♠ 9 8 6 2
    ♡ A K                                ♡ 7 4
    ◊ A K J 10 9 7 4   W  +  E           ◊ Q 2
    ♣ K                                  ♣ Q 8 5 4 2
                         S
                    ♠ 5 4
                    ♡ Q J 10 8 2
                    ◊ 8 6 3
                    ♣ 7 6 3
```

Jim lost a diamond and two hearts. There was no way to get to my partner to score her queen of clubs before Jim pitched them on his spades. "Oh well," I said to Claudia as Jim's partner tallied up the score for their vulnerable game, "I just pushed them to where they should have been anyway."

"I'll bet you five dollars no one was in that game," Jim said. "I only had three points."

"Don't you think I should have bid that?" Jim's partner asked.

"No," Jim said. "Carl had to have the ace and king of hearts and a stiff club honor. Those aren't very good odds."

Jim's partner showed us the travelling score with a smile on his face. There were several diamond contracts our way and one or two heart contracts their way. No one was in game. Unbelievable! Jim had done it to us again, or rather I had done it to us again. Jim finished first, and we dropped to an ignominious tie for third.

"My, my," Claudia said as we walked away from the table, "it never ceases to amaze me how much there is to learn about this game. Is that how you play for average?"

♠ ♡ ◇ ♣

# C H A P T E R   1 3
# Sheila

*If thou dost play with (her) at any game / Thou art sure to lose;*
*and of that natural luck /(She) beats thee 'gainst the odds.*
- With apologies to William Shakespeare

Do you have someone in your club who always, always manages to get the best of you at the bridge table...no matter what? For me, that person is Sheila.

Just the sound of her name strikes terror in my heart. Try as I might, I never seem to get a good board from Sheila. If there is a 27 point game that goes down at every table, Sheila will inevitably stop in a partial against us. A tough to find but icy slam? Sheila will just give one of her patented "oh what the heck" shrugs and bid it at our table. A killing lead? Watch out! That's Sheila reaching for a card. We all have our Sheila's, don't we?

Observe this board from a club game:

**VUL: BOTH      DLR: SOUTH**

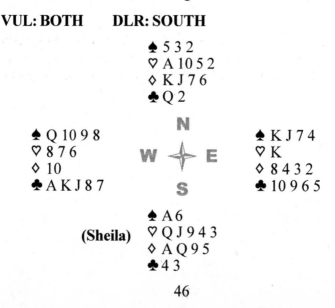

```
                    ♠ 5 3 2
                    ♡ A 10 5 2
                    ◇ K J 7 6
                    ♣ Q 2
                         N
   ♠ Q 10 9 8                        ♠ K J 7 4
   ♡ 8 7 6                           ♡ K
   ◇ 10          W  ✧  E            ◇ 8 4 3 2
   ♣ A K J 8 7                       ♣ 10 9 6 5
                         S
                    ♠ A 6
        (Sheila)    ♡ Q J 9 4 3
                    ◇ A Q 9 5
                    ♣ 4 3
```

After Sheila, sitting South, opened ONE HEART, her partner gave her a limit raise. Sheila carried on to FOUR HEARTS. I was sitting East. My partner led the ace and king of clubs. On the second club, I played the ten suggesting a spade switch. Partner led the 8 of spades, I played my King and Sheila took her ace. The critical moment had arrived. Sheila led her queen of hearts, and my partner played low. After only a moment's thought, Sheila called for the ace, and down crashed my singleton king.

"Well," Sheila said with a knowing smile, that's the first time that rule ever worked for me."

"Rule," I said. "What rule?"

"Eight ever, nine never."

How annoying.

"Wrong rule, Sheila," I said. "That's for not finessing and playing to drop doubleton queens when you have nine cards in the suit, not for dropping singleton kings! You need to check with me about these rules before you apply them."

Sheila only smiled and opened the scoreslip. Needless to say, FOUR HEARTS was down one at every other table. Sheila, however, was not finished with us yet. With more than a little apprehension, I picked up my next hand: ♠: 7 ♡: Q J 10 7 5 ◇: A 8 6 5 ♣: 10 7 6

Sheila, on my left, opened TWO HEARTS. My partner passed as did Sheila's partner. I had nothing to say and was happy with my heart stack. What could go wrong here? Alas, here was the entire hand:

**VUL: NONE      DLR: SOUTH**

```
                    ♠ A K 6 5 2
                    ♡ 9
                    ◊ K Q 3
                    ♣ K 4 3 2
   ♠ Q J 10 9            N              ♠ 7
   ♡ 8                                  ♡ Q J 10 7 5
   ◊ J 10 9 7       W  ✦  E             ◊ A 8 6 5
   ♣ Q J 9 8                            ♣ 10 7 6
                        S
                    ♠ 8 4 3
                    ♡ A K 6 4 3 2
                    ◊ 4 2
                    ♣ A 5
```

Sheila was South. When North put down the dummy, Sheila was very apologetic. "I'm sorry," she said. "I don't usually open a WEAK TWO if I have an outside ace and three of the other major. I don't know what got into me. We can surely make FOUR SPADES. I'm sorry."

I had trouble concentrating during the play of the hand thinking that for once I was going to get a good result against my nemesis. The splits in the majors were both terrible, however, and Sheila made just TWO HEARTS on the nose. Her partner opened the scoreslip, and incredibly all the other tables were in FOUR SPADES going down one or two.

"Very nice, partner," said North as he penciled in 110 into the North-South column, the only score there.

"Thank you," said Sheila.

I couldn't believe it. Sheila had done it to me again.

♠ ♡ ◊ ♣

# C H A P T E R   1 4
# Sheila's Revenge

*Sweet is revenge- especially to women.*
- Byron

Shortly after chapter 12 was published as a monthly column in the ACBL Bulletin, a number of us from our club traveled to the Topsfield, Massachusetts, sectional tournament for the Sunday Swiss teams. Sheila was there, and when we bumped into each other before the game, she acknowledged my column.

"Very nice story," she said with a mischievous glint in her eye.

Oh oh. I hoped we wouldn't have to meet her team that day. Fate, however, had both teams at average and brought us together for an after-dinner encounter. Luckily, Sheila wasn't at our table. She was in my seat at the other table, though. She would be holding my cards. Maybe that wasn't such a good thing either. Here was what I was dealt in the swing hand of the match: ♠: — ♡: A K 4 ◊: K Q J 10 9 7 5 2 ♣: J 4.

I was the dealer and considered opening some high number of diamonds, but I decided the hand was too strong. I opened ONE DIAMOND. West bid ONE SPADE. TWO CLUBS from my wife, Claudia. East passed and I bid THREE DIAMONDS. Undaunted, West bid THREE SPADES, and Claudia doubled. After some thought, I decided I had too many diamonds without the ace to leave in the double, so I bid FOUR DIAMONDS. Claudia carried on to game. After the opening lead of the king of spades, Claudia mumbled as she put down the dummy that she didn't think we had bid the hand correctly. Here was the entire hand:

**DLR: SOUTH    VUL: N-S**

```
                    ♠ Q 10 8 6
                    ♡ 5 3
                    ◊ A 4
                    ♣ A Q 10 9 8

  ♠ A K 7 5 4 3 2        N          ♠ J 9
  ♡ Q J                             ♡ 10 9 8 7 6 2
  ◊ 6 3          W  ✦  E            ◊ 8
  ♣ K 3                             ♣ 7 6 5 2
                        S
                    ♠ —
                    ♡ A K 4
                    ◊ K Q J 10 9 7 5 2
                    ♣ J 4
```

Don't worry," I told my wife after I took all 13 tricks, " we had nowhere near the points to bid slam."

When the round was over, we compared the results with our teammates.

"Plus 640," I said when we got to this board.

"Minus 1390," they said.

"What?" I said incredulously. "How on earth did they bid that?"

"Sheila opened FIVE DIAMONDS," our partner replied. "I bid FIVE SPADES, and Sheila's partner doubled. But Sheila couldn't stand the double with all of her diamonds, so she bid SIX DIAMONDS!"

Aargh! Sheila had done it to me again.

Later that evening, I told my sad Sheila tale to a player from Massachusetts that I knew. He was sympathetic, but he said that he had an even sadder tale to relate. They had lost a match when his partner opened a weak TWO SPADES, and some lady overcalled THREE HEARTS with only ♠: x x ♡: Q J x x x ◊: x x ♣: K Q x x. The lady's partner had an opening hand and, naturally, raised to FOUR HEARTS, which made. At the other table, his teammate reasonably passed with the heart hand. His partner balanced with THREE DIA-MONDS and played it there.

"Wait a minute," I said suspiciously. "Who was this lady that over-called with that heart hand?"

He looked around, found her, and pointed to a woman over on the far side of the room. "That's her," he said.

"Congratulations," I told him. "You just met Sheila.

# C H A P T E R   1 5
# She's Back!

*No one can escape his destiny.*
- Plato

I wrote about my early encounters with Sheila in 1995. I'm happy (?) to report that Sheila is still around, still wreaking havoc with my game.

One of Sheila's talents is slipping in and out of auctions unscathed, jamming the bidding but somehow never getting caught. Everyone knows that Sheila loves to shoot from the hip with her wild bids, but if you try to catch her, like a shadowy sprite, she's gone.

My partners, for example, will simply not allow me to double Sheila. Inexplicably, they always come to her rescue. Observe: ♠: Q 8 6  ♡: A Q  ◇: A Q 10 9 8  ♣: Q J 10. Playing with my brother-in-law Eric, I picked up this hand in first position at equal vulnerability. I opened ONE NO TRUMP, and Eric bid TWO CLUBS, Stayman. Sheila, on my right, reached for her bid box, but she was going for a bid card, not a pass card. Oh oh. What was coming? Incredibly, it was FOUR DIAMONDS! I happily doubled. LHO passed, and Eric...wait....Eric was starting to think. What could he possibly be thinking about?

ERIC, I tried to shout at him telepathically. WHAT ARE YOU THINKING ABOUT? MY DOUBLE IS FOR PENALTY. WHAT ELSE COULD IT BE? PASS! PASS!

But no. Eric, after a great deal of tortured thought, bid FOUR SPADES. Sheila smiled and passed, and the chance for one of the biggest penalty doubles of my life was gone.

More evidence:

**DLR: NORTH   VUL: NONE**

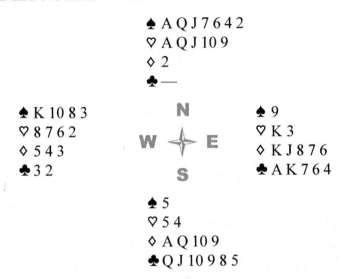

♠ A Q J 7 6 4 2
♡ A Q J 10 9
◇ 2
♣ —

♠ K 10 8 3
♡ 8 7 6 2
◇ 5 4 3
♣ 3 2

♠ 9
♡ K 3
◇ K J 8 7 6
♣ A K 7 6 4

♠ 5
♡ 5 4
◇ A Q 10 9
♣ Q J 10 9 8 5

My partner, new to our club, had quickly learned of Sheila's reputation. In fact, when she made a late appearance at our table for the round against us on this fateful night, he even joked, "so here comes the world's largest overbidder." Sheila just picked up her cards with a twinkle in her eye. My partner was sitting North, and this was the bidding:

| North | East | South | West |
|---|---|---|---|
| (partner) | (Sheila) | (Carl) | |
| 1 ♠ | 2NT | PASS | 3 ◇ |
| 3 ♡ | 4 ◇ ! | DBL | PASS |
| ??? | | | |

Oh no. It was happening again. My partner was thinking. What could he possibly be thinking about? Noooo! But, sure enough, he bid FOUR SPADES. There was Sheila's smile again and her pass card. Dazed and out of control, I bid FIVE HEARTS, my longer major. Partner now bid SIX CLUBS. What was he doing? I had no choice but to cue bid SIX DIAMONDS, and partner settled in SIX HEARTS.

The play was not a pretty sight, so instead I concentrated on what our score might have been in FOUR DIAMONDS DOUBLED. Sheila would have gone for a minimum of 800.

After the play was over, my partner gently admonished me. "If I freely bid game in my first suit," he said, "don't take me out of it."

Even more gently, I replied, "And if I double Sheila, don't take me out of that."

♠ ♡ ◇ ♣

# PART THREE
# The Bidding

Bridge, to the casual outside observer, must indeed look like a funny game. Bridge players bid in silence using a code that is limited to seven numbers and ten words in an attempt to convey the strength of their hands and the best strain in which to play them.

This would be a difficult enough proposition by itself, but bridge players are masochists- they add conventions to their arsenals of standard bids. A convention is a bid that is given a specialized meaning, usually contrary to its natural interpretation. There are artificial bids, relays, cue bids of the opponents' suits, western cue bids of the opponents' suits, Michael's cue bids of the opponents' suits, color cue bids of the opponents' suits, splinters, splinter jumps, fragments, and many, many more. In the upper echelons of bridge, there are even bids where a pass means that you have a bid, and a bid means you do not have a bid!

As Eddie Kantar says in his book *Bridge Conventions*, "more disasters than successes come from the use of a new convention until both partners understand it well." And even when both partners understand the convention, one of them will most likely forget it by the time it comes up at the table.

More bridge games are probably won or lost in the bidding than in any other aspect of the game. How well can you evaluate your hand? Can you judge whether or not you should be in a partial, a game, a slam, or a grand slam? How well can your opponents do that against you, and how often are you able to jam their bidding when they are on their way to the perfect spot? Do you balance once they've landed safely in their perfect spot? Do you sufficiently punish opponents who attempt to jam your bidding or balance you out of your perfect spot?

Needless to say, all of these coded conversations and coded interferences produce fertile ground for errors and misunderstandings. And that is all part of the fun of this very funny game. Here are some of my favorite stories about the bidding.

♠ ♡ ◇ ♣

C H A P T E R   1 6
# Understandings

*Wisdom is the principal thing; therefore, get wisdom: and*
*with all thy getting get understanding.*
*- Proverbs, The Bible*

Wouldn't bridge would be an easier game if our partners could simply talk to us and tell us what they have or what their bids and leads mean? Part of the fun of this game, however, is being limited to the handful of words that make up the language of bidding.

You are allowed to use the names of the four suits and no trump as well as the words pass, double, redouble- along with Alerts and Announcements. Unless your opponents ask for a further explanation of your bids, that's it. My philosophy is not to ask unless I really need to know, and then I only ask once the bidding is over. Nothing is more annoying than clearing up a bidding misunderstanding for your opponents while they are in the process of having it.

"Oh, thanks for asking," I have heard more than once. "I forgot we were playing that convention."

"Aarghh!"

Because the language we use has such a limited vocabulary, it is incumbent upon ongoing partnerships to discuss as many aspects of their bidding as possible. What does each one of your bids mean? Do the meanings change when there is interference? What conventions do you use? How do you handle those conventions over interference? Are systems on or off? In what situations would you cue bid an opponent's suit, and what do those cue bids mean?

What leads do you use? What about discards? Which ace-asking conventions do you use? Do you use Gerber, and if so, when? Is there any situation when a bid of 4NT would be quantitative rather than ace asking (1NT-4NT, for instance, which asks partner to bid 6NT if he is at the top of his point range)?

These are all things you should discuss ahead of time with your partner. It sounds tedious, but the few minutes you invest discussing your system will reap numerous rewards in your game.

Some of the game's top pairs spend hours on end discussing their complex systems in order to avoid any misunderstandings. I remember seeing one of New England's top players sitting at a table by himself between rounds going through a sheaf of papers he had taken from his pocket.

"That's quite a system," I said to him in awe.

"My partner leaves no stone unturned," he said.

We don't have to be quite that thorough, but whatever time we spend discussing our systems will be time well spent. The convention card is an excellent tool that most of us can use before a game to go over our understandings. Whenever my occasional partner from Vermont, Steve Bean, and I got together for a sectional tournament, we would meet for lunch first and go over our entire card point by point regardless of how many times we had done it before.

Even though we have had similar discussions, my brother-in-law Eric and I missed a crucial point that came up on this deal in a recent sectional Swiss Team event. The misunderstanding cost us a match against the top team in the field. In second position, I picked up: ♠: J 9 6 ♡: A K ♢: K 7 4 3 ♣: A Q 8 6. RHO passed, and I opened 1NT. LHO bid 2 CLUBS which was alerted as Brozel showing clubs and hearts. My partner Eric bid 3 CLUBS which was Stayman, and I bid 3 DIAMONDS showing no four card major.

Eric now jumped to 4NT. Hmm. We had just plunged into muddy waters. We played Roman Key Card Blackwood, but we hadn't agreed on a suit yet, had we? Or would it be diamonds, the last bid suit? Wouldn't he use Gerber, 4 CLUBS, to ask for aces, or was that only direct over a no trump opening bid? Eric and I were an occasional partnership, but I couldn't remember if we had discussed this point.

With my maximum 17 points, I decided I didn't want to miss a vulnerable slam, so I jumped to SIX NO TRUMP. After a slight hesitation, Eric passed. Here was the entire deal:

**DLR: EAST**      **VUL: NONE**

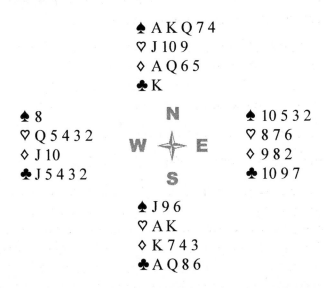

```
                ♠ A K Q 7 4
                ♡ J 10 9
                ◊ A Q 6 5
                ♣ K

♠ 8                              ♠ 10 5 3 2
♡ Q 5 4 3 2          N           ♡ 8 7 6
◊ J 10          W  ✦  E          ◊ 9 8 2
♣ J 5 4 3 2          S           ♣ 10 9 7

                ♠ J 9 6
                ♡ A K
                ◊ K 7 4 3
                ♣ A Q 8 6
```

We had all 13 tricks. West, of course, was just monkeying around, trying to gum up our bidding, and he accomplished just that. Our opponents at the other table, without any interference, had no trouble getting to the grand slam. The 500 point bonus for bidding it cost us the match which, amazingly, we would have won 7 to nothing if it hadn't been for this disaster. We should have gotten to the grand slam too, shouldn't we?

"You had 19 points," I told Eric. "Shouldn't you have just gone to seven after I showed a maximum?"

"Nineteen and seventeen is thirty-six," he said. "What if they had an ace? Why didn't you respond to Blackwood? Then I would have known."

"I thought Gerber would be ace-asking."

"That's only directly over no trump, isn't it?"
Later in the day, I asked Ron Mack, one of our opponents who was at the

other table and one of New Hampshire's top players, what we should have done. Wasn't 4NT in that situation quantity?

"Yes," he said, "four no trump is definitely quantity."

Ha. I couldn't wait to tell Eric.

"But," he continued, "if you accept the invitation to slam, you should show how many aces you have to help out partner as much as possible."

Good thought. I would tell Eric about it...later. Seriously, though, isn't this a conversation you should have with your partner now rather than after you've had a bidding misunderstanding?

# C H A P T E R   1 7
# A Round With The Expert

*An expert is one who knows more and more about less and less.*
- Nicholas Butler

My brother-in-law Eric has always enjoyed playing cards. He has a regular Thursday night poker game, he plays whist on his lunch hour at work, and his children are always challenging him to one card game or another. So when his sister and I got into duplicate bridge, he wanted in on the action. After a few quick lessons and a couple of games at our local club, I thought Eric was ready for his first sectional tournament.

Things went as smoothly as could be expected for our first few rounds. Then I noticed we were approaching the table of one of New England's top players. I informed Eric that we would be playing an expert, a person with thousands of masterpoints. Duly impressed, Eric sat down with an appropriately apprehensive look on his face. I picked up the following hand: ♠: K Q J 5 3 ♡: — ◇: 10 9 7 ♣: J 8 6 4 2.

This was a typical tournament hand for me. My interest was piqued, however, when the expert on my right opened the bidding in his deep-toned and urbane voice with ONE SPADE. This was in the days before bidding boxes, and the expert's voice and demeanor had always been intimidating to me. This time, though, I was sitting behind the expert with a fistful of his spades. I passed attempting to sound as disinterested in this deal as I possibly could be. The excitement continued to build when the expert's partner on my left bid TWO SPADES, which the expert alerted.

It was Eric's turn. He had a confused look on his face.

61

"What does that mean?" he asked.

"Constructive," the expert said. "Tends to be strong."

All right! Now I was really getting excited. Visions of doubling the expert's contract and getting a good board against him danced through my head. The bidding, however, had come to a stop. I glanced up from my wonderful spade holding to see Eric studying his cards intently. What could he be thinking? Certainly he didn't have anything to say. Come on, Eric, what are you doing? Pass! Then, it happened.

"FOUR NO TRUMP," Eric blurted.

"What?" I asked incredulously. Surely I hadn't heard him correctly.

"FOUR NO TRUMP," he repeated, this time with a confident smile.

The expert turned his head slowly in my direction

"What's he doing?" the expert asked.

"I have no idea," I said, flabbergasted. Certainly Eric had lost his mind. Why did it have to happen at this table?

"No bid," the expert said.

"What?" I asked.

"No bid."

I thought the expert was making some kind of ruling on my brother-in-law's bid of FOUR NO TRUMP.

"What do you mean?" I asked.

"Pass," the expert said, somewhat annoyed and obviously anxious to get on with what was going to be a slaughter of us two novices.

I looked with dismay at my cards and at that beautiful and now forever lost spade suit. What could Eric possibly be doing? Maybe he meant it to be unusual. Yes, that had to be it. I mentioned this to the expert, and he just nodded at me with a slight smile, ready to hammer whatever bid I was about to make at the five level. The five level.

So, responding to what I thought was the unusual no trump, I bid my longest minor which, luckily was clubs.

"FIVE CLUBS," I said tremulously.

"Pass," from the person on my left.

Then from Eric..."FIVE HEARTS."

"And what is he doing now?" the expert asked me.

"I don't know," I said with more than a little terror in my heart.

"Double" said the expert with finality.

We were dead. Was Eric cuebidding? No, I hadn't taught him cuebidding yet. What should I say? I stared at my cards hoping that somehow an answer would materialize. Alas, there was nowhere to run. Hopefully Eric would realize he had another bid and go back to clubs. I passed, LHO passed, and Eric just gave a shrug and passed as well.

The expert led a spade, and Eric claimed at trick two. His hand:

♠: —   ♡: A K Q J 10 9 8 7 6 4 2   ◊: 3   ♣: 5

"Isn't FOUR NO TRUMP Blackwood," he asked me, somewhat annoyed that I, his mentor, had missed the bid.

"Well, yes, I guess it is," I said.

"If you had an ace, I was going to bid slam."

"What if I had the ace of spades?"

"I don't know. Maybe they'd lead spades and I'd get a pitch."

Fortunately, my longer minor had been clubs. Five diamonds would have told Eric that I had one ace!

That evening at the dinner break, we compared hands with our friends. Everyone was in some number of hearts–four or five, making five; or six hearts going down one. We were the only pair in five hearts doubled.

To this day, Eric still likes to tell the story of the top he got against an expert.

♠ ♡ ◇ ♣

C H A P T E R   1 8
# Down The Middle

*If we would guide by the light of reason,*
*we must let our minds be bold.*
- Louis Brandeis

My most memorable moment in bridge was the result of a bid I made in one memorable hand at a sectional tournament in Stratham, New Hampshire. To the vast majority of bridge players, it might not seem like such a thrill for it only gave our team a fourth place finish in the Sunday Swiss Team event. At the time, however, we were four novices with less than 200 points between us. This tournament was also back in the days of unstratified events, so we were competing against everyone. I think that many accomplished players have forgotten the thrill of doing well on just one hand against players who are far superior to them. The four of us will certainly never forget what happened on this one deal against...Lester.

Before I tell you about Lester, let me describe the path that brought us to that fateful moment in Stratham on that Sunday. My wife Claudia and I along with friends Elizabeth and Steve Bean from Vermont had entered the unflighted event with few expectations. The field was over 80% life masters, so we all agreed that this day was going to be just for fun. Sure. How many times have you said that about bridge, and how many times have you actually had fun? Bridge is simply not much fun when you're getting hammered.

We won our first match by a reasonable margin, however, and our second with a blitz. We found ourselves in second place and playing the tournament leaders- a team that included former ACBL President Ed Gould and his wife. Pretty exciting stuff for four novices. On the second board, with favorable vulnerability, I picked up: ♠: K Q J 8 5 3 ♡: Q 9 ◊: 7 5 2 ♣: Q 4. Mrs. Gould on my right opened ONE NO TRUMP. I jumped into the fray with a bid of TWO SPADES, and Mr. Gould on my left went into a tank. I mean, I have never seen a pause so long before or since at the bridge table. Mrs. Gould squirmed. Claudia coughed hoping, I think, to startle him out of his trance. I began to wonder what I had done or if the man was having a stroke. Finally, he bid TWO NO TRUMP, which his wife alerted as Lebensohl. We didn't know what that was and passed throughout. Somehow, the Goulds got tangled in their bidding and wound up in a contract of FOUR NO TRUMP, down one! We lost the match regardless, but this swing kept us close and the margin of victory was only two IMPS. We thought that would be our big thrill of the day. Wrong!

Round four was a close loss to another good team, but in round five we were crushed by a weaker team. At the dinner break, we were more than satisfied with our two wins and our score of dead average. We speculated how many we might win in the evening session. Little did we know what was in store for us. We blitzed our first match and won our second handily.

"We're back up with the big boys now," Steve said to me when he returned with our assignment for the final round. Our wives had stepped outside for some air. "Don't tell the girls," he continued. "It'll only make them nervous. We're in fifth place right now. Let's see if we can hold onto it. Just play it down the middle."

Claudia and I went over to our assigned table, and she knew immediately that something was up when she saw who was sitting there waiting for us...Lester, one of the top players in the field.

"What's going on?" she asked.

"We're in fifth place," I said. "They're third."

"Oh no," she said, and I could see her tensing up.

"Don't worry. We'll be fine," I said trying to sound as reassuring as I could. "Just play it down the middle."

Now, let me tell you a little about Lester. He had over three thousand master points. He wore only jeans and a T-shirt to all events, and when he had to give some thought to a hand, he would chew on the sleeve of his shirt, which was extremely distracting for Claudia. When Lester was declarer, he took about ten seconds to look over the dummy, and then he played the cards in rapid fire succession, peeling them out of his hand and slapping them on the table, a veritable waterfall of winners spilling out of his hand too quickly for us to follow.

"Flat hand," he said after the play was over. "No squeeze possible."

Needless to say, we were in awe of Lester.

I picked up my cards from the first board of the match and stared at the most incredible collection of clubs and diamonds I had ever seen. The only problem was the paucity of points: ♠:— ♡: 4 ◊: J 8 6 5 3 2 ♣: J 10 9 8 5 3.

I was in first position. I had two thoughts. Steve told us to "play it down the middle," but Frank, my first bridge teacher, had always said "bridge is for the bold." I looked at my two points and all those clubs and all those diamonds. We weren't vulnerable. I had to bid. I couldn't help it.

I opened ONE DIAMOND. TWO DIAMONDS (Michaels') from Lester on my left. THREE DIAMONDS from Claudia. What had I stirred up? FOUR HEARTS from RHO. I couldn't stop now. I bid FIVE DIAMONDS. If looks could kill, I wouldn't be writing this now. In Claudia's hand were the ace, king and queen of hearts and the ace of diamonds. She was ready to double FOUR HEARTS, but in this amazing hand, FOUR HEARTS would have made four! Pass from Lester and an agonized pass from Claudia. But, from RHO...FIVE SPADES. Here was the entire deal:

**DLR: SOUTH    VUL: E-W**

```
              ♠ 7 6 5 4
              ♡ A K Q
              ◇ A 10 9 7 4
              ♣ Q
  ♠ A K Q 10 8      N        ♠ J 9 4 2
  ♡ 10 9 7 6 2                ♡ J 8 5 3
  ◇ —          W  ✦  E       ◇ K Q
  ♣ 7 6 2          S         ♣ A K 4
              ♠ —
              ♡ 4
              ◇ J 8 6 5 3 2
              ♣ J 10 9 8 5 3
```

When Claudia took her ace, king and queen of hearts, I saw Lester jot a minus 100 on his personal scoresheet. He scratched that out and wrote in minus 200 when his partner took a ruffing finesse and Claudia scored her ace of diamonds. At the other table our partners made FOUR HEARTS doubled.

Swing hand. We beat Lester and his mates handily and wound up third overall. I still wonder what would have happened to my biggest thrill in bridge if I had not been bold and "played it down the middle."

C H A P T E R   1 9
# Reputations

*A bad reputation is like a hangover. It takes a while to get rid of it,
and it makes everything else hurt.*
- James Preston

The origin of the word "reputation" can be traced to Middle English. "Re" means "again" and "Puten" is "to think. Apparently our ancestors behaved consistently enough so that their fellows thought about them in the same way they had thought about them before. Thus, our ancestors acquired reputations.

Today we do the same at the bridge table. We would like to think that every bid and play we make is original and unpredictable, but of course that's not the case. We fall into patterns, and we acquire reputations. Some of us are overbidders, some underbidders.; some are sacrificers; some play in no trump regardless of ten card trump fits; some will always, always take the bait and bid one level higher in a competitive auction, while others will surrender meekly. Some will open light, and others can be counted on for a solid 13 count with every opening bid.

Opportunities abound to use an opponent's reputation to your advantage. With some players you can balance aggressively and then wait confidently while they take the bait, bid one level too high and go set. With other players, however, if you stick your neck into their auction, it's the guillotine for you. It pays to know which pairs are which. Be aware of your opponents' reputations. Observe this hand which I picked up as dealer in first position at a recent club game: ♠: Q J 9 3 ♡: 3 2 ◇: K Q J 8 7 6 3 ♣:—

As dealer, I passed. I did not want to preempt in diamonds because I held four spades. LHO opened ONE DIAMOND. Hmmm. Interesting. RHO bid ONE SPADE. I liked the way this auction was proceeding. I passed again, and LHO bid TWO DIAMONDS. RHO now bid THREE CLUBS, and LHO settled into what she thought was a comfortable contract of THREE NO TRUMP. This was passed around to me. I, however, knew LHO's reputation. She did not like to let her opponents think that they had her trapped in the wrong spot. She would always try to wriggle out. I knew, just knew what would happen if I doubled, so I gave it a try. Sure enough, LHO gave her partner an annoyed look and confidently bid FOUR DIAMONDS!

I did not double this contract. LHO had six diamonds and I had the rest. Par on the board was some high number of diamonds declared by MY hand, doubled by LHO, and going set for minus 500 or 800. By the way, they would have made THREE NO TRUMP!

The downside of reputations, though, is that you have one too, and you can't help bringing it with you to the bridge table. Look what happened to me on this deal from a game at our club:

**DLR: WEST    VUL: NONE**

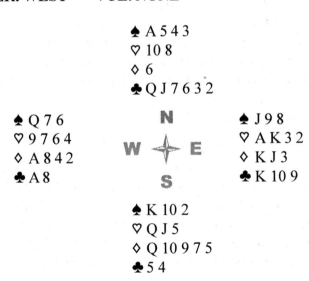

```
                    ♠ A 5 4 3
                    ♥ 10 8
                    ◊ 6
                    ♣ Q J 7 6 3 2

  ♠ Q 7 6              N              ♠ J 9 8
  ♥ 9 7 6 4                           ♥ A K 3 2
  ◊ A 8 4 2      W  ✦  E              ◊ K J 3
  ♣ A 8                               ♣ K 10 9
                     S
                    ♠ K 10 2
                    ♥ Q J 5
                    ◊ Q 10 9 7 5
                    ♣ 5 4
```

I was South. Our opponents were a charming retired couple for whom bridge was as much an opportunity for an evening of socializing and fun as it was a contest. In case you didn't know it, this type of opponent is the most dangerous to someone who takes himself seriously at the bridge table. East, the wife, opened ONE CLUB in third position. Her husband responded ONE DIAMOND, after which she passed! What would you have done? Certain that they had made an egregious error and were handing us a top, I was more than happy to pass with my little fistful of diamonds. My wife Claudia led the 10 of hearts.

"Oh, oh," I thought when I saw the balanced fifteen point dummy. This was not going to be an average board. West made ONE DIAMOND on the nose. I did not want to look at the traveling score. Sure enough, the field was in THREE NO TRUMP or FOUR HEARTS going down one or two.

"I didn't have another bid, did I?" East asked my wife sweetly.

"Well," she suggested, "you could have bid one heart."

"Oh no," said East. "I know my husband. He'd think I had five hearts if I said that, and he'd get all excited."

"How about ONE NO TRUMP?" I offered.

"No way," she said. "I've been stung too many times with that bid. And besides," she added, "you'd double anything I bid anyways. I know your reputation. You weren't getting me to bid again. Look dear, we got a top. Well played."

♠ ♡ ◇ ♣

# CHAPTER 20
# Key Card For Key Largo

*We had it all / Just like Bogey and Bacall*
*Starring in our own late, late show*
*Sailing away to Key Largo.*
- Bertie Higgins, *"Key Largo"*

One of the delights of playing duplicate bridge is the ability to find a game practically anywhere. Whether you're on business or vacation, there is almost certain to be a bridge club nearby.

One winter several years ago, Claudia and I were vacationing in the Florida Keys. Sure enough, there it was in our ACBL Club Directory-the Key Largo Duplicate Bridge Club. So, off we went- Bogie and Bacall on our way to Key Largo.

What better convention to have added to our convention card for this occasion than Roman Key Card Blackwood. It's not that difficult to learn, and when the right hand comes along, it can really improve the accuracy of your slam bidding.

Here's how it works: The king of trumps counts as an ace, so now there are five aces, or key cards, instead of four. The responses to FOUR NO TRUMP in Key Card are

| | |
|---|---|
| FIVE CLUBS = | zero or three key cards |
| FIVE DIAMONDS = | one or four key cards |
| FIVE HEARTS = | two or five key cards without the queen of the agreed suit |
| FIVE SPADES = | two or five key cards with the queen of the agreed suit |

The king of trumps is almost as important as an ace. With Key Card Blackwood, you can easily find out if you are off both an ace and the trump suit king; if so, then bidding slam would be against the odds. Key Card also allows you to find out about the queen of trumps, a nice feature when you are thinking about bidding a grand slam.

After the response to 4NT, a 5NT rebid guarantees all five key cards and asks for kings, excluding the king of trumps which you already know about. You can respond to 5NT by bidding specific kings up the line (5NT-6D, for example, shows the king of diamonds and says you do not have the king of clubs), or you can simply show the number of other kings you have by bidding up the line (5NT-6D would then show one additional king).

Of course, to use Key Card, you must have agreed on a trump suit. If you haven't, assume the last-bid suit is trumps. That's all there is to it. (For further applications or variations, consult *Modern Bridge Conventions* by Bill Root and Richard Pavlicek).

Here's how Key Card worked for us in Key Largo. I held: ♠: Q 9 8 7 4 ♡: A K Q 8 4 ◇: A ♣: K J and opened ONE SPADE. Claudia responded 2NT, which I alerted as a game-forcing spade raise. In our system, this shows an opening bid or more and guarantees four trumps but no singleton or void. Some players show strong major suit raises with only three trumps, but we think it's important to guarantee a fourth trump. Here was the entire auction:

| *Bacall* | *Bogie* |
|----------|---------|
|          | 1 ♠     |
| 2 NT (1) | 4 NT (2) |
| 5 ♣ (3)  | 5 NT (4) |
| 6 ♣ (5)  | 7 ♠ (6) |

(1) Strong spade raise with 4 trumps and no singleton or void
(2) Key Card Blackwood for spades
(3) Zero or three key cards
(4) Any other kings?
(5) No
(6) It doesn't matter. I can't picture many hands where this won't be cold kid!

This was the full deal:

```
              ♠ A K 6 5
              ♡ 7 3
              ◊ Q 4 2
              ♣ A Q 8 4

♠ J 3              N              ♠ 10 2
♡ 9 6 5                          ♡ J 10 2
◊ K J 9 7 5 3   W  ✦  E          ◊ 10 8 6
♣ 10 9             S             ♣ 7 6 5 3 2

              ♠ Q 9 8 7 4
              ♡ A K Q 8 4
              ◊ A
              ♣ K J
```

I won the opening club lead in my hand, played two rounds of trumps and claimed when the opponents both followed. Everyone bid slam, but only one other pair bid the grand.

As is usually the case with bridge players when there is a grand slam on one of the boards, that was the subject of conversation after the game.

"Did you bid the grand?" I overheard one player ask another.

"No. I was worried about the quality of my trump suit. I only had five to the queen-nine."

You won't have any such worry if you use Key Card. When you learn that partner has the ace AND THE KING of trumps, bidding this grand slam is easy- especially if you happen to be in Key Largo.

"Nice bid," my Bacall said to me as I claimed.

"Here's looking at you, kid," I replied.

Oops! Wrong movie.

♠ ♡ ◊ ♣

# CHAPTER 21
# Pressure

*Luck? Sure. But only after long practice
and only with the ability to think under pressure.*
- Babe Didrikson Zaharias

Bridge players must learn to make decisions under pressure. Often the pressure comes in the form of a preemptive bid that is made against you.

Observe this hand which I held in second position at a club game: ♠: K ♡: A Q J 5 ◊: K J 10 9 8 6 ♣: A 4. A nice looking hand until my right hand opponent opened THREE CLUBS. Good grief! Now what? My brother-in-law Eric was my partner, and I knew that if I doubled, he would bid spades and I'd never hear the end of it. But what if we had a heart fit? Well, if he bid spades, I would just have to bid my diamonds.

I doubled, West passed, and Eric took out his Stop card, announcing a skip bid. Oh, oh. Here it comes. I closed my eyes, but when I opened them, Eric's FOUR HEART bid card was lying on the table. Whew!

Only one other pair was in hearts making four. Every other South overcalled in diamonds, down two. There were five diamonds to the ace-queen on my left.

As we tallied the score, LHO razzed me for my "anti-percentage takeout double." Even Eric, who had tied for a top because of my double, joined in (he's my brother-in-law after all). I was just lucky. What if he had jumped in spades which was much more likely than his heart bid?

I was vindicated, however, when I showed the hand to one of our club's top players. The preempt, he agreed, had put me under pressure. Under the circumstances, my best action was to double.

My favorite example of bidding under pressure was from a Swiss teams match recounted by my friend Steve. Steve was sitting South, and his LHO was an old nemesis of ours, Captain Bic.

In fourth position, Steve held: ♠: A K 7 6 4 2 ♡:— ◊: A K 6 4 3 2 ♣:5. A very nice two-suiter, but Captain Bic, dressed in his dapperly manner, opened a strong TWO CLUBS in first position. Now what? But wait. Steve's partner was reaching for his bidding box. Incredibly, he placed the TWO SPADES bid card on the table. RHO passed. What would you do with Steve's hand? Steve decided to apply a little pressure of his own. He jumped to SIX SPADES.

Undaunted, Captain Bic, his multi-tiered row of pens displayed impressively in his breast pocket, took out the SEVEN CLUBS card. Two passes to Steve. Now what?

Reasonably enough, Steve doubled hoping that his partner would take it as a Lightner Double and find a heart lead for him to ruff, or that one of his aces would cash. Alas, North led a diamond, and here was the entire hand:

**DLR: WEST      VUL: BOTH**

```
                    ♠ Q J 10 9 8 5
                    ♡ 9
                    ◊ 8 7 5
                    ♣ 10 3 2
  ♠ —                   N            ♠ 3
  ♡ A K Q 8 6 5                      ♡ J 10 7 4 3 2
  ◊ —             W  ✦  E            ◊ Q J 10 9
  ♣ A K Q J 8 7 4       S            ♣ 9 6
                    ♠ A K 7 6 4 2
                    ♡ —
                    ◊ A K 6 4 3 2
                    ♣ 5
```

Who could blame North for not leading his singleton heart to give South a ruff? How could he possibly know East-West had an undisclosed twelve card heart fit? Captain Bic ruffed the diamond lead and said, "Well boys, I think all the tricks are mine."

At the other table, Steve's partners were in SEVEN HEARTS doubled for only a 4 IMP swing. They lost the match by 10 IMPS. If Steve doesn't double, it's 8 IMPS, and they still lose the match. Do you see the winning action? I showed this hand to many players, and only one came up with the right answer...bid SEVEN SPADES with Steve's hand. This player said he had taken lessons with world champion Karen McCallum, and Karen said that with a hand like South's that included the controlling spade suit, the opponents would never get to play the hand, no matter what the level.

SEVEN SPADES doubled only goes down two for minus 500 and an 18 IMP swing. But how many of us would have bid SEVEN SPADES under the pressure of Captain Bic's SEVEN CLUB bid?

♠ ♡ ◇ ♣

C H A P T E R  2 2
# The Fix

*At least in wrestling you know the fix is on; in boxing you can
never tell until Don King has a smile on his face and more
money in his pocket.*
- Benjamin Trecroci - *The Columbia Chronicle*

It all seemed so innocent. My partner and I were having a decent
game. A couple of boards looked to be below average at the
time, but all the rest seemed good, and there were a number of tops. We
had visions of placing in the local duplicate, maybe even finishing first.
The last pair, Dot and Gert, two pleasant ladies apparently bearing no ill
will towards us, came to our table. Little did we know that the fix was on.

Charles Goren *in Goren's New Bridge Complete* defines "fixed" as
"given a bad score through no fault of one's own." When you are on the
receiving end of a fix, however, that definition seems euphemistic indeed.
A fix takes away whatever wind was in your sails and leaves you dead in
the water. Any thought you had of placing is now just a distant memory.

Observe this three board set with Dot and Gert. Our heretofore
decent game was about to be left in shambles. On the first board, Gert
was in 3NT. After my partner's lead, she only had eight tricks. When we
got in, we had the contract set. Gert ran 3 club tricks, then played the ace
of spades and another toward KQ10 in the dummy. My partner
played low and Gert began to think. Oh no. My remaining spades were
the 8 and the 5. Sure enough, she finessed the 10. No one else
made 3NT.

"How did you dare to finesse that 10?" my partner asked.

"Because if I hadn't I wouldn't have made it, would I?" Gert replied.

On the second board, Dot was in the spotlight. She was South.

**Dlr: South Vul: N-S**

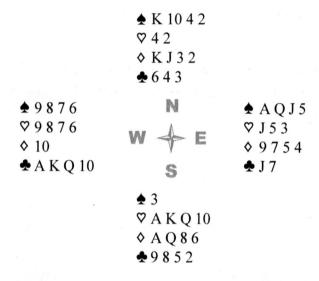

```
                    ♠ K 10 4 2
                    ♡ 4 2
                    ♢ K J 3 2
                    ♣ 6 4 3
     ♠ 9 8 7 6           N            ♠ A Q J 5
     ♡ 9 8 7 6                        ♡ J 5 3
     ♢ 10          W  ✦  E            ♢ 9 7 5 4
     ♣ A K Q 10        S              ♣ J 7
                    ♠ 3
                    ♡ A K Q 10
                    ♢ A Q 8 6
                    ♣ 9 8 5 2
```

She opened 1 Diamond. Gert said 1 Spade. Ignoring her singleton, Dot bid 1NT because, she told us later, she didn't like her clubs well enough to bid them. Sitting West, I took the first four club tricks then shifted to the 9 of spades. Dot covered with the 10, and my partner won the jack. Reasonably, she shifted to a heart. Dot took the rest of the tricks, making TWO NO TRUMP for a score of 120.

"Where did her other spade go?" asked my crestfallen partner.

"She had a singleton," I said woefully. "Everybody's making 110 in diamonds. If you cash your ace of spades, we hold her to 90 and a top for us, but why would you ever think that's the right play?"

That was two zeros. The third board saw Dot open 1NT with ♠: A x x ♡: K Q x x ♢: K x x ♣: K x x. Gert's hand was: ♠: K Q x x ♡: x x x ♢: x ♣: A Q x x x . Gert bid 2 Clubs, Stayman. Dot replied 2 Hearts. Gert then bid 2 Spades and everyone passed. Two spades made three. Suffice it to say that the room was in 3NT. None of the suits split and everyone was going down.

"Why did you bid 2 Spades with only four of them?" my dazed partner asked.

"Well," Gert said, "I didn't expect her to pass!"

"Nice bid," Dot said.

"Yes, thanks," Gert said with a smile on her face. "I didn't think we were having much of a game tonight, but now I think we might really have a chance."

♠ ♡ ◇ ♣

C H A P T E R  2 3
# Interference

*The sole end for which mankind are warranted, individually*
*or collectively, in interfering with the liberty of action of*
*any of their number, is self-protection.*
- John Stuart Mill

No, John Stuart Mill was not a bridge player, but a 19th century philosopher and economist. His philosophy of interfering, however, would serve the aspiring 21st century tournament bridge player quite well indeed.

Players who sit back and allow their opponents to have their way at the table without interference will be players who lose. Self-protection in the world of tournament bridge demands that you interfere with your opponents as much as possible.

Frank Stewart says that players hate to see "busy bidders" come to the table. Busy bidders are nuisances who can sometimes cause their opponents to lose their way in their auctions. Observe the following two hands from a New Hampshire sectional.

In first position I picked up: ♠: 10 6 4 ♡: A 9 7 2 ◇: 9 ♣: A Q 8 7 3. I passed, and LHO opened 1 Diamond. My partner passed and RHO bid 1 Heart. Here was my chance. My vulnerable opponents, both fine players, were well into an uninterrupted auction. Left to their own devices, they would surely find the right spot. We were not vulnerable, so I bid 2 Clubs. LHO bid 2 Diamonds, and my partner bid 3 Clubs. Oh, oh. I cringed in anticipation of the impending DOUBLE. RHO passed, however, and LHO bid 3 Diamonds. All pass. Making four.

So, you wonder, what did all of this risky bidding by me and my partner accomplish? Here was the entire deal:

**VUL: E-W**     **DLR: South**

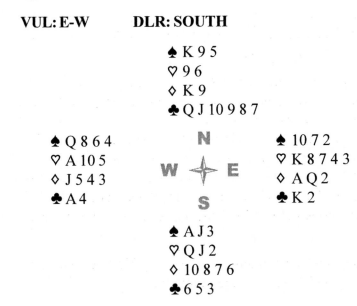

♠ J 7
♡ Q J 10 6
◇ 10 8 7 3
♣ K J 9

♠ A 9 8 3
♡ 5
◇ A K Q 6 5 2
♣ 10 5

♠ K Q 5 2
♡ K 8 4 3
◇ J 4
♣ 6 4 2

♠ 10 6 4
♡ A 9 7 2
◇ 9
♣ A Q 8 7 3

"Should I have done anything else?" RHO asked her partner.

"Nothing you could do," he said. "Bad board for us. We're cold for four spades."

Whether or not they bid game, our opponents would have been +170 or +620. Against us they were +130 giving us a tie for top.

Later in the same session:

**VUL: E-W**     **DLR: SOUTH**

♠ K 9 5
♡ 9 6
◇ K 9
♣ Q J 10 9 8 7

♠ Q 8 6 4
♡ A 10 5
◇ J 5 4 3
♣ A 4

♠ 10 7 2
♡ K 8 7 4 3
◇ A Q 2
♣ K 2

♠ A J 3
♡ Q J 2
◇ 10 8 7 6
♣ 6 5 3

My partner opened 3 Clubs in third position. This makes it all but impossible for our opponents to stop in their safe heart partial. At our table, East passed and we were -50 for a next to top. If you are wondering about my partner's lack of a seventh club, I was a passed hand, and the vulnerability was right. If you only interfere with your opponents when the conditions are perfect, or if you worry too much about getting doubled and going for an occasional big penalty, then your opponents might be just a little too happy to see you coming to their table. Be a busy bidder. Be a little more unwelcome. Have fun!

♠ ♡ ◇ ♣

# C H A P T E R   2 4
# The Best Game - Part I

*If you don't know where you are, you're nowhere.*
- Gilbert Grosvenor

In order to be a successful duplicate bridge player, you have to understand the nature of the beast. Players who have played bridge- in some cases, for years- but have never played duplicate bridge have come to our club to play. They don't understand why they scored so poorly when their actions during the session seemed perfectly normal to them.

In *The Complete Book Of Duplicate Bridge* by Kay, Silodor and Karpin, the authors discuss the philosophy of duplicate covering everything from bidding games and slams, to part scores, sacrifices, and overtricks. In duplicate, the winner is "the one who obtains the best relative result with the cards which he has at his disposal." Thus, this philosophy unique to duplicate bridge must be taken into consideration if one wants to be a successful duplicate player.

One of the decisions faced by players during a session of duplicate is which game is best. Should you be in a minor suit, a major suit, or no trump? According to Kay, Silodor and Karpin, your attitude toward minor suit games should be one of contempt.

Why make eleven tricks in clubs if you can take the same eleven tricks in no trump? Only as a last resort should you be in the minor. Observe this hand which I picked up recently at the club: ♠: 9 6 2 ♡: 10 8 ◇: 7 ♣: A Q J 8 5 4 3. My partner opened ONE NO TRUMP. What would you bid? I raised him directly to THREE NO TRUMP. I figured I had seven tricks for partner if he held the club king or if the king was onside. Here was the entire deal:

**DLR: NORTH    VUL: N-S**

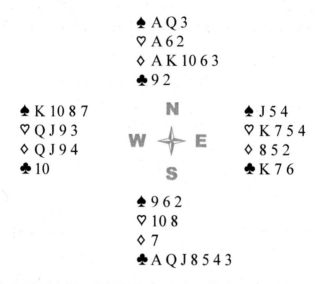

```
                    ♠ A Q 3
                    ♡ A 6 2
                    ◇ A K 10 6 3
                    ♣ 9 2
♠ K 10 8 7                          ♠ J 5 4
♡ Q J 9 3                           ♡ K 7 5 4
◇ Q J 9 4                           ◇ 8 5 2
♣ 10                                ♣ K 7 6
                    ♠ 9 6 2
                    ♡ 10 8
                    ◇ 7
                    ♣ A Q J 8 5 4 3
```

Partner got a heart lead which he ducked for two rounds in case the club king was offside and the hearts were 5-3. He then finessed the clubs twice and took the rest of the tricks. West looked at the traveler and moaned, "Of course they're all in clubs, making six. Some didn't even bid the game, and no one bid the slam." Then, as my partner scored up our top, West added, "We don't bid that way, do we partner? We would have been in clubs too, wouldn't we?"

Hmm. I did have a nagging doubt about my bidding, though. Were the odds in my favor with that kind of a bid? Later that night, I went on-line and e-mailed John Shuster, a Doctor of Statistics from the University of Florida, who had written to me numerous times about my columns and the bids and plays I had made in them. Who better to ask about percentages?

John wrote back that he thought I had bid the hand well. It was, he said, like a gambling 3NT except that I had the added advantage of knowing partner was holding a fine hand and at least two clubs. John said he once held: ♠: x  ♡: x x  ◇: A x x  ♣: A K Q 10 x x x. LHO opened THREE HEARTS, his partner overcalled THREE SPADES, and he bid

3NT eliciting the same kind of comment from his opponents when they found out he had no heart stopper. John reasoned that his non-vulnerable RHO had not gone on to FOUR HEARTS, so unless LHO had solid hearts, partner probably had a stopper. It turned out he had Kx. John got the ominous queen of hearts lead, but when he played the king, it held.

In my club hand, John said the odds were as follows:

| | | |
|---|---|---|
| 7 tricks: 47.5% | (K, K x, K x x onside) | |
| 6 tricks: 6% | (K, singleton, offside) | |
| 3 tricks: 2.5% | (K 10 x x offside) | |
| 2 tricks: 24% | (K x x  or K 10 x x offside) | |
| 1 trick: 20% | (K x offside) | |

Under the worst case, John said I was still a favorite because of overtricks in matchpoints. But even in IMPS, I had a lot of losers to take care of in FIVE CLUBS. According to John, there were two liabilities in bidding THREE CLUBS immediately:

> 1. I had no side stoppers, so how could partner's bid help me decide if there was an unstopped suit?
> 2. The next opponent may also have a long suit and make a lead directing bid at the three level.

Those all sound like pretty good odds to me. I, of course, am not good enough to calculate these percentages at the table. I think it's best to remember Kay, Silodor and Karpin's final bit of advice on the subject. About 95% of the time when a good minor "trump suit" is held, notrump should be the final contract. Those are odds that I can remember.

# C  H  A  P  T  E  R    2  5
# The Best Game - Part II

*If we could first know where we are, and whither we are tending,*
*we could better judge what to do and how to do it.*
- Abraham Lincoln

In Part I of "The Best Game," I talked about the necessity of understanding the philosophy of duplicate bridge in order to be a successful duplicate player. The idea of tournament bridge is to outscore all of the players who hold the same cards as you. As Kay, Silodor and Karpin say in *The Complete Book Of Duplicate Bridge*, "it's how well you exploit the resources that were bequeathed to you that will determine whether you end up a winner or a loser in duplicate bridge."

One of the problems that a duplicate player must deal with is which game to bid- a minor suit, a major suit, or no trump. In Part I, I told you about: ♠: 9 6 2 ♡: 10 8 ◇: 7 ♣: A Q J 8 5 4 3. If you are playing duplicate bridge and partner opens ONE NO TRUMP when you hold this kind of hand, the percentage bid is a direct raise to THREE NO TRUMP.

Another problem is whether to be in a major suit or in no trump. At IMPS, the safest game is an important consideration, but at duplicate another consideration is which game will score best.

In the same club session as the one in which I held the above hand, I also picked up: ♠: 8 3 2 ♡: K Q J 5 ◇: A 7 5 ♣: K J 9 and heard partner open ONE SPADE. What would you do? With my shapeless hand, I bid THREE NO TRUMP. I got a heart lead, RHO took the ace of hearts and continued hearts. The entire deal was:

**DLR: NORTH   VUL: N-S**

```
                 ♠ K J 10 9 5
                 ♡ 9
                 ♦ Q J 4
                 ♣ A Q 8 2
    ♠ 7 4              N              ♠ A Q 6
    ♡ 10 7 6 4 2·                    ♡ A 8 3
    ♦ K 10 8 3    W  ✦  E            ♦ 9 6 2
    ♣ 10 7              S            ♣ 6 5 4 3
                 ♠ 8 3 2
                 ♡ K Q J 5
                 ♦ A 7 5
                 ♣ K J 9
```

I lost the ace and queen of spades and the ace of hearts. Three no trump making four was a top. Some made four spades and some did not depending on whether they got a diamond lead. On any other lead, declarer can knock out the ace of hearts and pitch diamonds from his hand. But even those who made four spades scored 420 while the same tricks in no trump scored 430. What about my bidding, though? Was THREE NO TRUMP a percentage bid?

So, once again I e-mailed John Shuster, a doctor of statistics from the University of Florida for help. According to Dr. Shuster, probability was irrelevant on this hand. "The beauty of THREE NO TRUMP," said John "was that it concealed information. The expected heart lead, the weak spade suit and the lack of a doubleton made THREE NO TRUMP the spot of choice."

John was not surprised that FOUR SPADES failed. John said "the auction may go 1S-2C-3C-3S-4S. The choice of a red suit lead makes or breaks FOUR SPADES. THREE NO TRUMP is not cold, but it needs less to make."

Kit Woolsey in his book MATCHPOINTS says the hand with three card support is almost always better placed to choose the best game. If he is 4-3-3-3, no trump will probably produce the same number of tricks provided that the combined hands contain extra strength and all side suits are adequately stopped. As John Shuster said, however, if the hand with three card support also has a doubleton, then the 5-3 trump suit usually scores an extra trick.

Invest a little time to learn the strategy of duplicate bridge, and soon those occasional good boards will begin to add up to good games.

## C H A P T E R   2 6

# A Walk on the Wild Side - Part I

*Wild thing. You make my heart sing*
*You make everything groovy.*
- Chip Taylor

Nelson Algren's novel *A Walk on the Wild Side* is about Bohemian life in New Orleans, but it could have been a bridge book, couldn't it–a book about some of the hands and the players that make bridge the entertaining game that it is.

Part of the thrill of this great game is the wild hands that arise every so often and the wild things that some of those wild players do with those hands. What bridge player doesn't have a story to tell about some crazy distribution they have encountered, some 5-0 trump split, some eight or nine card suit or more, some double void?

There are some players who relish the flat boards, the average scores. They haven't blown any tricks. They haven't gotten a zero. They have done exactly the same as everybody else with the hand. What fun is that? If all boards were flat, who would come to bridge games?

Imagine this hand from our club recently. You are in third position, and you pick up: S: AKQJ987654 H: K D: 86 C: – Really! As you are wondering how you are going to bid this beauty, your partner (me!) opens the bidding in first position with ONE CLUB! What would you do? My partner Carol Leonard had heard enough. We were playing simple Blackwood, and she used it asking me for aces. When I replied that I had three, she simply bid 7 NO TRUMP. I never even had time to reverse with my own 17 points, but she figured she was looking at eleven tricks in her own hand. The opponents had ten hearts between them (luckily not eleven) for I had a void as well- spades , of course. Carol claimed 13 tricks at trick one. Some pairs were in SEVEN SPADES, and one even wallowed in SIX SPADES. The talk of the evening, though, was the ten card suit. How often have you seen that? What would you have done with it?

Many times the presence of a long suit, especially a minor, means that there will be some serious preempting in the bidding. Here's a memorable hand from a sectional a number of years ago. In third position at favorable vulnerability, I picked up: ♠: Q 7 ♡: 7 5 2 ◊: 9 ♣: Q 8 6 5 4 3 2. My partner opened ONE CLUB. My right hand opponent bid TWO CLUBS. I didn't ask for an explanation. I just figured it was time to jam the bidding at a high level, so I bid 5 CLUBS. East-West were about to have a massive bidding misunderstanding, and my 5 level bid would give them no room to recover. West, thinking that they were playing Michael's Cue bids which showed 5-5 in the majors, bid 5 SPADES, which my partner happily doubled. East, however, was cue bidding as a strong take-out. Here was the entire hand:

**DLR: N      VUL: E-W**

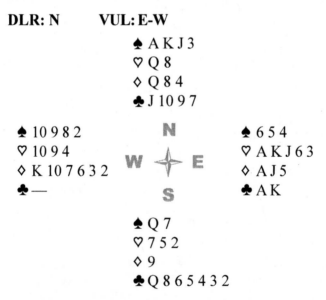

```
                    ♠ A K J 3
                    ♡ Q 8
                    ◊ Q 8 4
                    ♣ J 10 9 7

♠ 10 9 8 2              N              ♠ 6 5 4
♡ 10 9 4                               ♡ A K J 6 3
◊ K 10 7 6 3 2   W  ✦  E               ◊ A J 5
♣ —                    S               ♣ A K

                    ♠ Q 7
                    ♡ 7 5 2
                    ◊ 9
                    ♣ Q 8 6 5 4 3 2
```

My partner led the jack of clubs, and when dummy came down West just shook his head and said sadly, "We are sooo screwed."

We were plus 800 for a top. As you can imagine, this hand was all over the place. There were some minus 500, 800, and 1100's our way for 5, 6, and 7 CLUBS DOUBLED. East-West have chances for thirteen tricks in hearts, especially if South leads an unfortunate singleton diamond, so some Souths had apparently just kept on bidding...unable to control their wild sides.

There is little science here, but perhaps a lesson. When you have one of those long suits and you're going to preempt with it, take your one shot and then step aside. What is it the current take-out food commercial says? Get in, get out, get on with your life. The same applies to preemptive bidding. If your opponents land on their feet, so be it. You have done your best. Chances are, though, that their own wild sides might lead them astray.

# CHAPTER 27
# A Walk on the Wild Side - Part II

*The first blow is half the battle*
- Oliver Goldsmith

Wild hands, as we saw in the last chapter, are part of the fun of bridge. We also saw that oftentimes the presence of a wild hand means that someone is going to preempt.

The word "preempt" comes from the Latin "prae" meaning "pre" and "emers" meaning "to buy"- literally to buy ahead of time. When you preempt in bridge you make a higher than necessary bid hoping to shut out bids by the opponents and hoping that if any penalty is incurred, it is less than the value of the opponents' game, slam, or partscore.

Let's go for a walk on the wild side:

**DLR: WEST**    **VUL: N-S**

```
                    ♠ A J 7 3 2
                    ♡ A
                    ◇ A J 6 5
                    ♣ A K 10
  ♠ K 8                N              ♠ Q 10 6 5
  ♡ K 9 8 7 5 4 3 2              W      ♡ Q J 6
  ◇ 10              W  ✦  E        ◇ 8 4
  ♣ 9 2                              ♣ Q J 7 5
                       S
                    ♠ 9 4
                    ♡ 10
                    ◇ K Q 9 7 3 2
                    ♣ 8 6 4 3
```

I was South on this hand, playing with a new partner, someone who up until this deal had seemed relatively sane. Sitting West was a player who hated to be pushed around in the bidding and for whom it was anathema to allow the opponents to play in a contract with which they seemed satisfied. She also did not understand the virtue of preempting at the highest possible level as quickly as possible and then letting the opponents stumble from that point on.

There was a sitout that night at the club, and a kibitzer who had already played the hand sat down at our table and witnessed this incredible bidding:

| West | North | East | South (Me) |
|------|-------|------|------------|
| 4 ♡ | DBL | PASS | 5 ◊ |
| 5 ♡! | 6 ◊! | PASS | PASS |
| 6 ♡! | 7 ◊!! | PASS | PASS |
| 7 ♡!!! | DBL | ALL PASS | |

"I'm dizzy," the kibitzer said as she got up and left. At her table the bidding had simply gone 4 ♡, DBL, PASS, 5 ◊, ALL PASS. Quietly making five.

My partner, of course, should have doubled five hearts. Incredibly, West took the push and bid six hearts! We now had our top. But no. Partner had lost all semblance of control. West had a top if she had just passed. But no. Not this West. Do you think my partner would have bid EIGHT DIAMONDS if he could have?

Remember, fire your preemptive strike and then get out of the bidding. Get in, get out, get on with your life.

"Oh really," Claudia said to me as we were discussing this deal. "Why is it you don't take your own advice?"

"What do you mean?"

"The hand with my brother Eric."

"That was just bad luck," I said. "I could have been right."

**DLR: WEST     VUL: EAST-WEST**

```
                      ♠ 2
                      ♡ A K 2
                      ◊ 8 6 4 3
                      ♣ 8 7 6 5 3

   ♠ 4                   N              ♠ A K 7
   ♡ 10 9 6                             ♡ Q J 8 7 4
   ◊ A J 9 7 5       W  ✦  E            ◊ K Q 10
   ♣ A K J 10                           ♣ Q 9
                         S
                      ♠ Q J 10 9 8 6 5 3
                      ♡ 5 3
                      ◊ 2
                      ♣ 4 2
```

Eric, sitting West, opened ONE DIAMOND. Claudia, North, passed. East responded ONE HEART. We weren't vulnerable. It was time to strike. I, South, bid 4 SPADES.

Incredibly, Eric bid FIVE CLUBS. East bid FIVE DIAMONDS, and Eric now bid FIVE HEARTS! East raised him to SIX HEARTS. Up until this moment Claudia, sitting North, had no interest whatsoever in all of this bidding. Suddenly, when East bid SIX HEARTS, she was very interested. Unfortunately for her, I was next to bid and not her. With a smile on my face and not about to be pushed around by my brother-in-law, I reached for my bidding box and pulled out the SIX SPADE bid, confident that my sacrifice would cost less than their vulnerable slam.

Eric with a smile of his own doubled and led the ace of clubs. When Claudia placed the dummy gently on the table, one card at a time, there was much conversation when the Ace and King of Hearts appeared.

"Nice going," she said to me.

"Based on the bidding, you should have had those heart honors, shouldn't you?" East said to Eric.

"How am I supposed to know they lost their minds?" I said to any-one who would listen.

Claudia was right. My bid had done its damage. We had our top. Why was I bidding again? To avoid this kind of embarrassment, remember, when you're preempting, get in, get out, get on with your life.

# CHAPTER 28
# A Walk on the Wild Side - Part III

*A foolish consistency is the hobgoblin of little minds*
- Ralph Waldo Emerson

Emerson did not think much of people who were consistent. Consistency was for the small-minded. Emerson thought that those with great minds should dare to be different, change their minds when the situation called for it, and be individuals. Emerson would have loved bridge players, don't you think?

Haven't you ever marveled at the fact that given the same set of duplicated hands bridge players will inevitably come up with an astoundingly different set of results for those hands at different tables? The flat board with every result the same is the aberration, not the norm. Wouldn't you think it would be just the reverse?

One of my favorite Eddie Kantar stories about Yvonne was the one where she and a partner were playing North-South in a duplicate game. They played the first set of boards. When the new boards arrived, they passed them on and played the first set again. Different bidding, different results. Again, when the new boards came, they passed them on. Once more they began to play the first set, and once more there was different bidding, and a different result. This time, however, they called the director and complained someone had written on their line!

You can not accuse bridge players of being small-minded. Their actions, especially when it comes to dealing with those wild hands that show up occasionally, are as varied as their personalities. Observe this hand from a recent game at our club. What is your opening bid in first position with: ♠: — ♡: K Q J 10 8 7 4 2 ◊: A 7 2 ♣: Q 7 ?

Some players chose ONE HEART, and some opened with FOUR HEARTS hoping to shut out the spade bidders even though it might be their own partners. Whichever bid you chose, the fun was only beginning. Here was the entire deal:

**DLR: WEST     VUL: N-S**

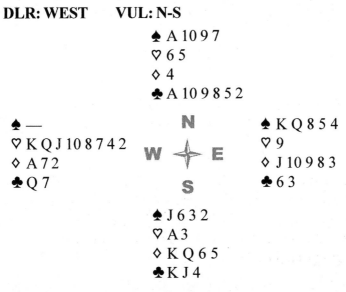

```
                    ♠ A 10 9 7
                    ♡ 6 5
                    ◇ 4
                    ♣ A 10 9 8 5 2

♠ —                           ♠ K Q 8 5 4
♡ K Q J 10 8 7 4 2            ♡ 9
◇ A 7 2                       ◇ J 10 9 8 3
♣ Q 7                         ♣ 6 3

                    ♠ J 6 3 2
                    ♡ A 3
                    ◇ K Q 6 5
                    ♣ K J 4
```

If West opens ONE HEART, do you take any action with the North hand? Do you bid TWO HEARTS, a slightly eccentric Michael's Cue bid showing spades and a minor, TWO CLUBS or do you make an even more eccentric take-out double? Would you bid with the East hand if North takes any action? And what about the South hand?

As you can see, at our club, all of these actions were taken at one table or another producing the eight different results listed here:

| CONTRACT | RESULT | N-S SCORE | N-S MP'S |
|---|---|---|---|
| 4 ♡ by W | DOWN 2 | 100 | 5 |
| 4 ♡* by W | DOWN 2 | 300 | 7 |
| 3 ♡ by W | DOWN 1 | 50 | 4 |
| 2 ♡ by W | MADE 2 | -110 | 3 |
| 3 NT by E | MADE 4! | -430 | 1 |
| 3 ♠ by S | DOWN 2 | -200 | 2 |
| 3 ♣ by N | MADE 3 | 110 | 6 |
| 4 ♠* by S | DOWN 3 | -800 | 0 |

Is there a lesson to be learned from this? Perhaps it's that conservatism pays off. The West TWO HEART bidder and the North 3 CLUB bidder were both above average. But what about the bold East who bid 3NT? Apparently North-South led and persisted in spades and never found the switch to clubs.

When someone does have a wild hand, it's important for the opponents to find the right defense. Here's another hand from our club:

**DLR: WEST      VUL: EAST-WEST**

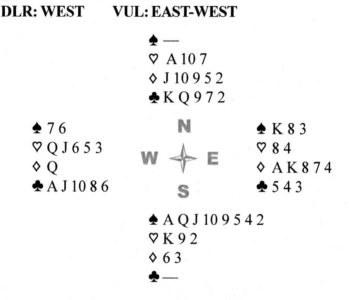

```
                    ♠ —
                    ♡ A 10 7
                    ◊ J 10 9 5 2
                    ♣ K Q 9 7 2

    ♠ 7 6              N           ♠ K 8 3
    ♡ Q J 6 5 3                    ♡ 8 4
    ◊ Q           W  ✦  E          ◊ A K 8 7 4
    ♣ A J 10 8 6       S           ♣ 5 4 3

                    ♠ A Q J 10 9 5 4 2
                    ♡ K 9 2
                    ◊ 6 3
                    ♣ —
```

I was South and there were three passes to me. What would you do? I opened 4 SPADES and everyone passed. West led her stiff queen of diamonds. Oh, oh. I had done it again. I could see two diamond losers, a heart loser and a spade. East did not overtake the diamond—would you?- and West was left on lead. What would you do now? She switched to a small heart, and my heart loser was gone. Amazing. Making four.

West fares no better leading the queen of hearts, for I can then finesse the jack. The ace of clubs is out. Do you see the winning play? A spade at trick two as long, of course, as East doesn't put in the king. I now can do nothing about my four losers. This should be a great result,

I thought. My partner, however, opened the traveller and announced "flat board."

Don't you just love bridge?

♠ ♡ ◇ ♣

# CHAPTER 29
# "X" Is For Double - Part I

*Double, double toil and trouble;*
*Fire burn and cauldron bubble.*
- William Shakespeare, Macbeth

Do you remember the first time you ever got doubled at the bridge table, when your opponent took out that ominous red card with the X on it and laid it on the table for all to see? For most of us it's a traumatic experience. I was once in a contract that was cold but managed to find a way to go down after I got doubled.

I also recall doubling my right hand opponent, who was a newer player, in a contract of THREE SPADES. After my double, the bidding went: PASS, PASS, FOUR SPADES! I doubled again, and this was down one! He would have made THREE SPADES doubled.

"Why did you bid FOUR SPADES after they doubled you in three?" LHO asked his partner.

"Because I didn't think THREE SPADES doubled was worth as much as bidding game," he said.

We've all gotten rattled at one time or another when we were doubled. Even worse, though, is when you double an opponent and he makes the contract. With several tricks to go, you can see the handwriting on the wall. You try to avoid your partner's glare, but you can feel it burning through your forehead.

"Making three," says your opponent.

"You were doubled too, weren't you?" asks his partner.

100

"Oh yes, that's right," he says cheerfully. "Carl doubled me. Let's see, that's double the points, plus the game bonus, plus 50 for the insult."

"No insult intended," you say, trying to add some levity to the situation, but your partner doesn't see the humor.

The thing to keep in mind, though, is that this is just a game, and in duplicate it's only one board. A zero is a zero is a zero. Period. They will not come and take away your first born child if you're responsible. At least they haven't come for mine yet.

Besides, you want to be an aggressive bidder in today's game, and you don't want to let the opponents push you around either. As the old bridge adage goes, if the opponents haven't ever made a doubled contract against you, then you're not doubling enough. That is certainly not one of my faults.

Here's part of my philosophy on doubles that has served me well over the years: if the hand belongs to you (you have the majority of the points) and two passed hands get to the two, or especially the three level, then double. Your opponents have kindly given you an opportunity for a top that others in your direction will not have. Seize that opportunity. Here is a case in point. I was sitting South for this deal:

**DLR: NORTH    VUL: ALL**

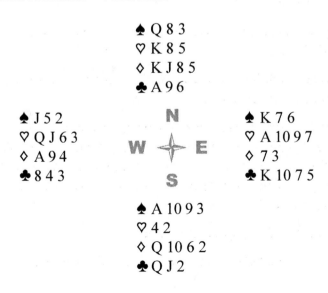

```
                    ♠ Q 8 3
                    ♡ K 8 5
                    ◊ K J 8 5
                    ♣ A 9 6

    ♠ J 5 2              N              ♠ K 7 6
    ♡ Q J 6 3                           ♡ A 10 9 7
    ◊ A 9 4         W  +  E             ◊ 7 3
    ♣ 8 4 3                             ♣ K 10 7 5
                        S

                    ♠ A 10 9 3
                    ♡ 4 2
                    ◊ Q 10 6 2
                    ♣ Q J 2
```

| North | East | South (Carl) | West |
|-------|------|--------------|------|
| 1 ◊   | PASS | 1 ♠          | PASS |
| 1 NT  | DBL  | ?            |      |

East, an otherwise kindly fellow, had annoyingly entered our auction in spite of his vulnerability. Partner had opened in first seat and I had nine points. The hand belonged to us. Had East not interfered, we would have quietly made one or two no trump for 90 or 120 points. East, however, had stepped into the cauldron and had to be punished for his transgression. I redoubled to show that I had more than a minimum hand. West bid TWO HEARTS, and my partner doubled. This was passed out, and my partner led a diamond.

West won the second diamond and led the queen of hearts. The key to this hand is for both sides to avoid breaking the spade suit. West could have succeeded by leading a club at trick three setting up the long club for a spade pitch. We would have had no answer to this line; West would have only lost two clubs, a diamond and two spades.

If he had done this, it wouldn't have much mattered. Minus 670 for TWO HEARTS doubled making two would have been almost as bad for us as minus 110 if we had not doubled, for most pairs would be making 90 or 120 our way. And, if we hadn't doubled and he goes down, plus 100 would still lose to the plus 120's our way.

As it was, partner covered the second heart putting West on the board. He could have still succeeded by leading a low club off the board. Instead, though, he tried a spade. I played low, and he put in the jack hoping I had the queen and partner the ace. Wrong! We now took 3 spades, 2 clubs, and a diamond for plus 200 and a top. Perhaps the kindly fellow sitting East wouldn't be so quick to enter our auctions in the future.

Here's another hand that belonged to us, but the opponents interfered and got overboard:

**DLR: WEST** **VUL: NONE**

```
                    ♠ A 10 2
                    ♡ K Q 7 5
                    ◇ J
                    ♣ A J 10 6 2
♠ K Q 5 4             N            ♠ 9 8
♡ 10 9 8                           ♡ A J 6 4 3 2
◇ Q 10 9      W ✦ E                ◇ 7 5 2
♣ Q 7 3               S            ♣ 9 4
                    ♠ J 7 6 3
                    ♡ —
                    ◇ A K 8 6 4 3
                    ♣ K 8 5
```

I was South. West passed. My partner opened ONE CLUB. East overcalled a weak 2 HEARTS. I made a negative double showing the other two suits. West bid THREE HEARTS, unwise with his flat distribution. But hey, you're not responsible for your opponents' bids, are you? Three hearts was passed around to me. What would you have done?

Once again, the opponents have stepped into the cauldron. You shouldn't have to wait for Horace to tell you to seize the day. Game is unsure, the hand definitely belongs to your side, and a passed hand and a preemptive one have gone to the three level, so you should double.

Partner has the option to take out your double, but in this case he is happy to leave it in. The opponents lose two diamonds, a ruff, one heart, one spade, and two clubs.

Down three is plus 500 for your side when the most you can make is plus 400 if you even get to game.

So remember, if your opponents get unruly in a deal that belongs to your side, don't let their transgressions go unpunished.

♠ ♡ ◇ ♣

# "X" Is For Double - Part II

*Protection is not a principle, but an expedient.*
- Benjamin Disraeli

Doubles are protection that you take out against the theft of something that rightfully belongs to you. Your opponents have sacrificed against your contract. They do not expect to make their bid, but they hope that their minus score will be less than the value of your contract. If they are correct, they will beat everyone in their direction who allows their opponents to play the contract.

For instance, you bid to a vulnerable heart game worth 620 points. Your non-vulnerable opponents (aren't they annoying?) bid on to four spades which they hope will go down no more than two or three tricks. You have to decide whether or not to bid on to five hearts. If you don't, then you must double their contract to protect what was rightfully yours. If several pairs find the sacrifice, you will at least get some matchpoints for doubling.

The second possibility is that the opponents have taken a phantom sacrifice. Your contract was going down all along, so now instead of plus 50 or 100, your opponents will be minus 100 or 300, and you will have a top rather than a bottom. Once again, it is expedient to double. If other pairs have taken the same phantom sacrifice, you do not want to lose any matchpoints by not doubling. Or, if other pairs your way are only in a partial, you still need to double to protect against the 140 they will score.

The third reason to double an opponent's sacrifice bid is that it is an opportunity for a top that other pairs your way might not have. The penalty for doubling their sacrifice might be greater than the value of your game. I've been on the wrong side of that one more often than I would care to remember, haven't you? "Sorry partner," you say with as much nonchalance as you can muster, "that was one too many."

Kit Woolsey in his book *Matchpoints* says that successful sacrifices usually net only a slightly above average matchpoint score, while an unsuccessful one virtually always gets a bottom. Still, many players today are sac-happy, refusing to allow you to play your contract. And, if it's against me, the sacrifice more often than not is one that works. You must remember to double, though. Sometimes the reward will surprise you.

Here was a hand from a recent game at my club. See what you would have done. I was dealt: ♠: A 5  ♡: A 9 6 2  ◊: 10 8 7 5 4 ♣: K 9 . I was South in second position. We were vulnerable and the opponents were not. RHO opened ONE CLUB. I passed as did LHO. Partner bid TWO SPADES, and RHO asked me for an explanation. I said we had not discussed this bid, but I thought that it was a good hand with at least six spades. I didn't think he had enough, however, to double and bid again. RHO then bid THREE CLUBS. With my two aces and well-placed king of clubs, I decided to bid FOUR SPADES.

LHO now came to life with FIVE CLUBS. This was passed around to me. What would you have done? Here was the entire hand:

**DLR: EAST      VUL: N-S**

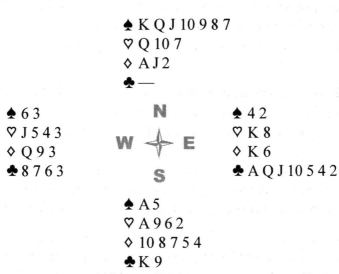

```
                    ♠ K Q J 10 9 8 7
                    ♡ Q 10 7
                    ◊ A J 2
                    ♣ —

  ♠ 6 3                N              ♠ 4 2
  ♡ J 5 4 3                           ♡ K 8
  ◊ Q 9 3         W  ✦  E             ◊ K 6
  ♣ 8 7 6 3                           ♣ A Q J 10 5 4 2
                      S

                    ♠ A 5
                    ♡ A 9 6 2
                    ◊ 10 8 7 5 4
                    ♣ K 9
```

Not everyone in our direction bid game, but everyone made five spades for either 200 or 650 points. I had no way to know this, however, so with my two aces and defensive club trick, I doubled. My partner did well to leave this in. He knew I was a passed hand and had no way of knowing if we would make five. He figured I must have had some club tricks. Besides, this was an opportunity for a top that other pairs might not have.

As you can see, they lost two spades, two hearts, a club, and a diamond for 800 points. With his flat hand, West's bid was at best a reckless gamble. He must have figured his partner for a singleton spade or no club losers, but he had no way of knowing that for sure. But, hey, as I've said previously, you aren't responsible for your opponents' bids. The only thing you must remember is to seize the opportunity with a double.

"Sorry partner," said West after the dust had cleared. "That was one too many."

Ah, isn't it sweet when the opponents have to make that statement and not you?

# C H A P T E R   3 1
# "X" Is For Double - Part III

*Heat not a furnace for your foe so hot*
*That it do singe yourself.*
-William Shakespeare, Henry VIII

There are plenty of times when you should double: to protect yourself against sacrifices, to punish the opponents who have entered your auction when the hand belongs to you, and to seize the opportunity for a top board which other pairs in your direction might not have.

There are just as many instances, however, when you should refrain from doubling. With the May 3rd hand from the 2003 Daily Bridge Calendar, Eric Kokish and Beverly Kraft demonstrate that "a double that tells declarer how to make the contract is foolish; a double that steers him from a doomed contract to one that makes is beyond foolish."

The hand is a heart slam in which one opponent holds all five of the outstanding hearts to the king and queen. That opponent doubles, and declarer runs to SIX NO TRUMP making twelve tricks by taking two finesses in another suit, stripping the hand and then throwing in the poor defender who holds all the hearts. He must now lead away from his second heart honor to yield declarer's twelfth trick. If declarer had not been doubled, he certainly would have gone down.

Do not double the opponents if (1) you are happy with their current contract, which you are reasonably sure you will set and (2) if they have a safe haven to which they can run if you do double. Check out this hand which came up recently at my club:

♠: A 4  ♡: K J 10 9 8 3  ◊: A 4  ♣: J 7 6.

I was South. East was my brother-in law Eric. He opened ONE SPADE, and I overcalled TWO HEARTS. West made a negative double, and my partner jumped to FOUR HEARTS. Eric now bid FIVE CLUBS. I didn't think we would take any heart tricks on defense, so I took the push to FIVE HEARTS. There were two passes, and Eric now bid FIVE SPADES. What would you have done with my hand?

Based on the bidding, I thought I could picture setting FIVE SPADES. My partner might have a singleton or void in clubs. I would lead a club and probably score my two aces and a ruff, or possibly two ruffs. Right? Was I happy? Of course not. East was my brother-in-law, remember? And the brother-in-law rule is that you inflict the maximum amount of punishment at the bridge table, so naturally I doubled. West immediately bid SIX CLUBS, which was again passed to me. Hmm. Would both my aces cash? Should I double? These questions were irrelevant, for here was the entire deal:

**DLR: EAST    VUL: NONE**

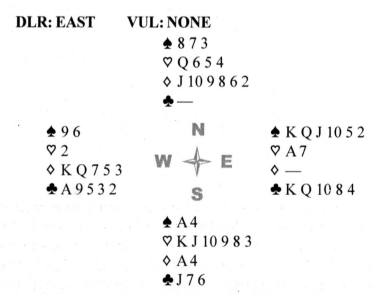

```
                    ♠ 8 7 3
                    ♡ Q 6 5 4
                    ◊ J 10 9 8 6 2
                    ♣ —
    ♠ 9 6                          ♠ K Q J 10 5 2
    ♡ 2              N             ♡ A 7
    ◊ K Q 7 5 3    W   E           ◊ —
    ♣ A 9 5 3 2      S             ♣ K Q 10 8 4
                    ♠ A 4
                    ♡ K J 10 9 8 3
                    ◊ A 4
                    ♣ J 7 6
```

My double of FIVE SPADES had pushed the opponents to where no other pairs had gone- to a cold SIX CLUB contract.

I led the ace of diamonds. Eric ruffed, drew trumps, placed a spade on the table and claimed. I could take my ace and that was it. The second part of the brother-in-law rule is that you will always push your brother-in-law to his best spot. FIVE SPADES down one would have been a good board for us, but I had ignored the fact that they had a safe haven, a club contract where there would be no ruff, and I foolishly doubled.

A few weeks later against one of our club's top pairs, I remembered the lesson:

**DLR: W**       **VUL: N-S**

```
                    ♠ 3
                    ♡ A 8 7 6 5 4
                    ◊ A Q 8 3
                    ♣ K 7

  ♠ A 10 8 7 4           N          ♠ K J
  ♡ K 9                             ♡ Q 2
  ◊ J 10 6       W  ✦  E            ◊ K 5
  ♣ Q 4 2                           ♣ A J 9 8 6 5 3
                        S

                    ♠ Q 9 6 5 2
                    ♡ J 10 3
                    ◊ 9 7 4 2
                    ♣ 10
```

| West | North | East | South |
|------|-------|------|-------|
|      |       |      | (Carl) |
| PASS | 1 ♡ | 2 ♣ | PASS |
| 2 ♠ | 3 ♡ | 3 ♠ | ? |

I'm not timid about doubling, especially when my partner has opened, my opponents get to the three level, and I hold five of their trumps. Two thoughts kept me from doubling, though. One: this was a top pair, and with the help of a double, West just might make THREE SPADES. Two: the opponents had a safe haven- clubs. I couldn't double that, so I passed.

West lost two spades, a heart and a diamond- making three, for a top...for us!

East can easily take eleven tricks in clubs and ten in no trump. So remember, don't try to burn the opponents with a double when they have somewhere to run and can turn the heat back on you.

♠ ♡ ◇ ♣

# C H A P T E R   3 2
# A Game Of Errors

*If we could be twice young and twice old,*
*we could correct all our mistakes.*
-Euripides

"**B**ridge is a game of errors" we've been told many a time after one of our numerous bridge blunders. So true. Dorothy Truscott in *Bid Better, Play Better* says "Naturally it's impossible to cut out all mistakes. The expert hasn't been born who doesn't make some. The average player probably makes about one hundred mistakes in bidding and play during an afternoon of bridge. Fortunately for his self-esteem he usually will recognize only about one per cent of them."

One thing Truscott failed to mention, however, is that some players seem doomed to repeat the same errors over and over.

When Claudia and I first took up the game, she had a mental block about the strong TWO CLUB opener. Inevitably she would open TWO CLUBS with 6-11 points and six clubs. She knew she was doing it and knew it was wrong, but out it would come anyways..."TWO CLUBS." Whenever this happened, the other players at the table would look in befuddlement at their cards and never figure out what was going on. I, of course, had to proceed as if she knew what the bid meant. Had she forgotten again, or not? I threatened to buy a T-shirt with WE PLAY TWO CLUBS STRONG emblazoned across the front.

It was encouraging for us, therefore, to see players who were better than we were make errors of their own and, yes, even repeat those errors. Observe this deal from a club game:

**Dealer: South    Vulnerable: North-South**

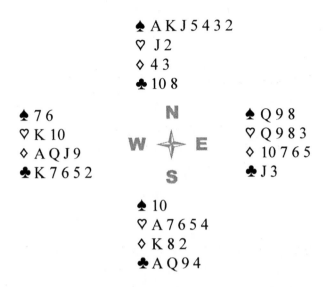

```
                    ♠ A K J 5 4 3 2
                    ♥ J 2
                    ◇ 4 3
                    ♣ 10 8

    ♠ 7 6              N              ♠ Q 9 8
    ♥ K 10                            ♥ Q 9 8 3
    ◇ A Q J 9     W  ✦  E            ◇ 10 7 6 5
    ♣ K 7 6 5 2                       ♣ J 3
                    S

                    ♠ 10
                    ♥ A 7 6 5 4
                    ◇ K 8 2
                    ♣ A Q 9 4
```

South, a fine player, opened ONE HEART. Claudia, sitting West, overcalled TWO CLUBS. North bid TWO SPADES. I passed, and South bid TWO NO TRUMP. THREE SPADES from North, and from South THREE NO TRUMP. Claudia's opening lead was the nine of diamonds implying two higher honors. South won and played the ace and king of spades. After that, no matter how she wriggled and squirmed, she had to go down 300 for a top for us. South berated North for not bidding FOUR SPADES, and North retorted that South had no business bidding THREE NO TRUMP with her minimum hand.

Unfortunately for North and South, this wasn't the end of the story. Incredibly, the following week at the club this board did not get shuffled. Even more incredible, the same four people sat down to play it. The exact same bidding ensued with South confidently settling into THREE NO TRUMP. Claudia made the same lead, but this time when the dummy was tabled South recognized that long string of useless spades.

"Hold on," she said. "I've played this." She called the director to complain, but the board had already been played twice. He said there was nothing he could do. Of course, he should have thrown out the board, but directors do not always make the correct ruling. "I'll tell you one thing," South said glaring at me, "I'm not playing the top spades. You have three to the queen." Sure enough, West was only down two. Only tied for bottom this week instead of dead bottom.

"You should have bid FOUR SPADES," South berated her partner. Again.

"You had no business bidding THREE NO TRUMP with that minimum," North retorted. Again.

Same deal. Same bidding. Same argument. Poor South. If there is an eternal punishment for bridge players, this could be what it is like- making the same mistakes over, and over, and over...

♠ ♡ ◇ ♣

C H A P T E R   3 3
# Concentration

*Depend on it, Sir, when a man knows he is to be hanged in a*
*fortnight, it concentrates his mind wonderfully.*
- Samuel Johnson

If only we could bring that kind of concentration to the bridge table! Perhaps more than any other attribute, the ability to concentrate is the one that would help the aspiring bridge player the most.

How many times, half way through the play of a hand, have you forgotten how the bidding went, what the opening lead was, who played which card, if a particular card had been played, what your opponent's first discard was, or even, heaven forbid, what your partner's first discard was?

How many times have you been on the receiving end of one of these post-mortems?

"A spade," partner says. "Why didn't you lead a spade?"

"I thought you wanted a club," you say.

"No," says partner. "My first discard was the two of clubs. The two!"

"I missed it," you say sheepishly.

Some nights our excuse is we have other things on our minds. Other nights, we think we are ready to play, but for some reason the focus just is not there. There's no doubt about it, if we could concentrate more on the game, we would all be better players.

Alas, I even manage to lose my concentration during the bidding sometimes going so far as to not notice what I have just bid. At a recent club game, I pulled out the following hand in first position:

♠: A Q 8 7 5  ♡: K Q 4  ◇: K 9 6  ♣: 10 9

I opened ONE SPADE. My wife, Claudia, responded ONE NO TRUMP, which I announced was forcing. I got odd looks from everyone at the table, but no one said anything. The opponents were silent. I bid TWO DIAMONDS, my first suit that was at least three cards in length. Claudia announced this as a transfer and bid TWO HEARTS. What was she doing? This wasn't a transfer. Hopefully, she really had hearts. I had nowhere to go, so I passed.

After our bidding cards were picked up, East asked me why I alerted Claudia's ONE NO TRUMP bid.

"We play ONE NO TRUMP FORCING," I said.

"What do you mean?"

When I open one of a major," I said, somewhat annoyed for I knew East was aware of what ONE NO TRUMP FORCING meant, "ONE NO TRUMP by her is forcing for one round."

"But you didn't open," he said. "You passed."

"No, you've got it wrong," I said, terror beginning to rise in my voice, "I opened ONE SPADE."

"No," Claudia said, "you've got it wrong. You passed."

She had opened ONE NO TRUMP and thought my diamond bid was a transfer to hearts! It didn't take Claudia long to claim all thirteen tricks. Later, one of the other players came up to me.

"Hey Carl," he said. "How did you guys manage to stop in TWO HEARTS on that grand slam hand?"

In another memorable hand in a recent Swiss Match at a sectional tournament, I picked up:

♠: 6 4  ♡: A 9  ◇: J 8 7  ♣: K Q 9 8 6 5

My partner opened ONE NO TRUMP, 15-17 points. I had ten points and a good club suit, so I bid THREE NO TRUMP. A spade was led.

"I hope you've got the ace of clubs," I said and tabled the dummy.

Partner did have a spade stop and the ace of clubs. Eleven tricks were easy. No probable swing on this hand. We couldn't make six clubs, could we?

"Nice card your ace of clubs," I told partner.

"Yes," he said. "How come you didn't bid THREE NO TRUMP?"

"What do you mean?" I said with a chuckle and a bit of a tremble. "I did bid THREE NO TRUMP."

"No," my right hand opponent said cheerfully, "you only bid TWO NO TRUMP."

I glanced desperately at the table for corroborating evidence, for the THREE NO TRUMP CARD that I had surely taken out of my bid box, but the bid cards, of course, had long since been put away.

Noooooo!

So you see, concentration doesn't only apply to declarer play and defense. It must begin when you take your first bid card (be sure you know what that card is!) out of the box and place it on the table in front of you.

# C H A P T E R   3 4
# Greed

*So for a good old-gentlemanly vice,*
*I think I must take up with avarice.*
        *- Byron "Don Juan"*

The grand slam. Just mention those words, as Frank Stewart says, and the bridge player gets a wistful gleam in his eye with a trace of awe and terror mixed in. When it comes to slams, however, the duplicate bridge player should proceed with caution and not get too greedy.

Small slams in duplicate should be 50% propositions or better. Grand slams should be 55% or better. Failure to reach a grand very rarely results in getting a zero, but reaching a grand and going down is almost a sure zero. If the slam is dubious, you will probably score as well if you just bid game and bring home twelve or thirteen tricks.

I remember a spade game at a long ago regional where the thought of a slam briefly crossed my mind, but I settled in game. Alas, there was a side suit that could be set up before drawing trumps, and I took all thirteen tricks. At dinner, a friend of mine said he knew, just knew he should have bid the slam. He easily scored twelve tricks, he said. When I got back from the break and checked our scores, I had an absolute top for taking 13 tricks. No one had bid the slam.

I wish I had considered all of this at the club last week when I picked up: ♠: A 10 9 8 2  ♡: A 9 6 2  ◇: 9  ♣: A K 9

My partner opened ONE NO TRUMP. We play 15-17 point no trumps. Hmm. I bid 3 SPADES showing a 5 card suit and 15 or more points. My partner bid 4 SPADES showing at least 3 card spade support.

116

Wow! My hand revalued to 17 points in support of spades, so I tried FOUR NO TRUMP, which was Key Card Blackwood. Partner answered 5 SPADES which showed two keycards (one ace and the king of spades) and the trump queen. I bid 5 NO TRUMP, and he bid 6 HEARTS showing the heart king and denying the diamond king. Enough! I bid 7 SPADES, which I had in mind all along, and got a trump lead. Here is what I saw:

```
        ♠ K Q 5
        ♡ K 10 6
        ◊ A Q J 10 8
        ♣ 8 7

              N

        W  ✛  E

              S

        ♠ A 10 9 8 2
        ♡ A 9 4 2
        ◊ 9
        ♣ A K 9
```

Oh, oh. I drew two rounds of trump, then played the ace and king of clubs and ruffed a club. I then played a heart to the ace and drew the last trump. Where would the two losing hearts in my hand go? I decided that I had to find the diamond king with East. I played a diamond to the ace and led the queen. East played low. I pitched a heart and closed my eyes. When I opened them, the five of diamonds was on the table. Phew!

Making seven. Here was the entire deal:

```
                    ♠ K Q 5
                    ♡ K 10 6
                    ◇ A Q J 10 8
                    ♣ 8 7

     ♠ J 7 4            N            ♠ 6 3
     ♡ J 8                           ♡ Q 7 5 3
     ◇ 6 5 4        W  ✦  E          ◇ K 7 3 2
     ♣ Q 10 6 3 2      S             ♣ J 5 4

                    ♠ A 10 9 8 2
                    ♡ A 9 4 2
                    ◇ 9
                    ♣ A K 9
```

"Nicely played," said my partner, " but I won't comment on the bidding."

"I made it, didn't I?"

"That'll just encourage you in the future."

He opened the traveler. Everyone was in 3NT or FOUR SPADES. No one had even bid a small slam, and two of the pairs in spades had only made 6! Bidding just game and making seven would have been tied for top. My greed to bid the grand had gambled all of the matchpoints for just one extra point.

♠ ♡ ◇ ♣

# C H A P T E R   3 5
# The Law

*I fought the law and the law won.*
- Sonny Curtis

In 1992, Larry Cohen published a book that changed the world of bridge.

Based on a 1969 article in Bridge World Magazine, Cohen's *To Bid or Not to Bid* explains the importance of the total number of trumps in competitive auctions. A bookseller at a regional tournament recommended the book to me. "It will change your game forever," he told me.

The basis of the book is simple. The Law of Total Tricks states: *The total number of tricks available on any deal is equal to the total number of trumps.* There are many adjustments and applications to this law, but you can improve your competitive decisions if you only remember THE LAW.

You have ♠: K 9 6 5 ♡: 8 6 ◇: A 8 4 ♣: Q 4 3 2. Partner opens ONE SPADE. RHO overcalls TWO HEARTS. You bid TWO SPADES. LHO annoyingly bids THREE HEARTS, which is passed back to you. Your side has nine trumps. That means it is safe to contract for nine tricks and bid THREE SPADES. Switch one of your spades with a club or a diamond. Now you only have eight trumps, and you should pass.

An important bidding maxim associated with THE LAW is: *The five level belongs to the opponents.* It's not important that you understand the math behind the maxim. Just remember it. "There have to be a lot of trumps," says Cohen, "for both sides to consider contracting for 11 tricks. If you can make 11 tricks in hearts, chances are they can only take 8 tricks in their suit. Doubling them is almost always a better decision than bidding on."

I know all that. I read the book. So why did all this happen at the club recently?

I was South holding ♠: A 6 ♡: J 10 4 2 ◊: 7 5 4 ♣: A J 9 8. My partner opened ONE SPADE. I said ONE NO TRUMP, forcing. LHO overcalled TWO CLUBS. Partner now said TWO HEARTS. I jumped to FOUR HEARTS. West, however, was not finished. He bid FIVE CLUBS! Ah. West was going for a long, sad ride in 5 CLUBS, doubled. But wait. I never had a chance to double. Partner was reaching for her bid box. She placed the 5 HEARTS card on the table. Her hand was: ♠: J 9 4 3 2 ♡: A K 6 5 ◊: A K 6 3 ♣:— With her club void she was happy to bid FIVE HEARTS, but when the dust cleared she was happy she was only down two.

After we left the table, I explained that seldom is bidding 5 over 5 correct. "It's part of the law of total tricks," I said.

So where was I on this deal two tables later?

**DLR: WEST    VUL: N-S**

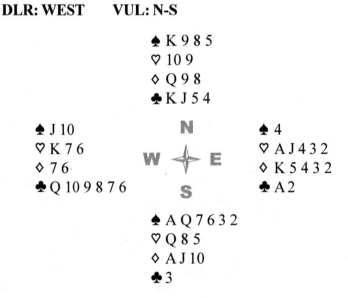

```
                ♠ K 9 8 5
                ♡ 10 9
                ◊ Q 9 8
                ♣ K J 5 4
  ♠ J 10              N              ♠ 4
  ♡ K 7 6                            ♡ A J 4 3 2
  ◊ 7 6        W  ✧  E              ◊ K 5 4 3 2
  ♣ Q 10 9 8 7 6       S            ♣ A 2
                ♠ A Q 7 6 3 2
                ♡ Q 8 5
                ◊ A J 10
                ♣ 3
```

In third position, East opened ONE HEART. I overcalled ONE SPADE. TWO HEARTS from West. My partner bid THREE HEARTS showing a limit raise or better in spades.

East passed and I bid FOUR SPADES. West and North both passed, but East now came in with an undisciplined FIVE HEARTS.

Two thoughts crossed my mind. East was stealing a vulnerable game from us, and my partner had to be short in hearts, maybe even void. So I bid FIVE SPADES. Down one for a zero.

. "I should have realized we had done well just to bid game," I told partner after the round. "FOUR SPADES making four would have been a tie for top. Plus 500 against FIVE HEARTS doubled gets us a next to top, and we even have chances for +800."

"Yes," my partner agreed. "What was that you told me about some law?"

# C H A P T E R   3 6
# Look Back In Anger

*If you are patient in one moment of anger,*
*you will escape a hundred days of sorrow.*
- Chinese Proverb

S toicism was a Greek school of philosophy founded in 308 B.C. by a teacher named Zeno. He taught that all things are governed by unvarying natural laws and that the wise man should follow virtue alone, obtained through reason, remaining indifferent to passion or emotion.

Good advice for the bridge table, don't you think? How many times has the rest of your game been affected by a bad board, a bad (or so you thought) bid or play from partner, or a fix from the opponents? I can remember one such instance that cost us a sectional win. This wasn't just a section top or a single game- it would have been our first two session sectional overall win.

After the first session, we were in first place, one point ahead of a flight A pair who probably won these things in their sleep. We chalked up our 64% game to good fortune and had no expectations for the second session. At night, however, it began to happen again. Tops were raining down on us like manna from the heavens. We were bidding and bringing home close games and slams, staying out of the impossible ones, and not missing a trick on defense. Then came board 11. In first position, I held:

♠: 10 9 8   ♡: A K 7 5   ◇: A Q 5   ♣: 10 4 2

I opened ONE DIAMOND. LHO overcalled ONE HEART. Partner bid THREE DIAMONDS. We play inverted minors, so this bid was preemptive, intended to jam the bidding. RHO bid THREE HEARTS. I passed as did LHO. Partner thought for a second, and then bid FOUR

DIAMONDS! Oh no. His preempt had already done its work. He shouldn't have bid again. FOUR HEARTS said RHO with confidence. I couldn't believe it. I was so angry with partner that I doubled. I had three sure tricks in hand, didn't I? Partner must have something. Alas, here was the entire hand:

**Dlr: South**          **Vul: None**

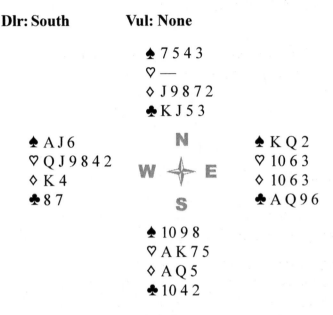

```
                    ♠ 7 5 4 3
                    ♡ —
                    ◊ J 9 8 7 2
                    ♣ K J 5 3

  ♠ A J 6              N              ♠ K Q 2
  ♡ Q J 9 8 4 2                      ♡ 10 6 3
  ◊ K 4          W  +  E             ◊ 10 6 3
  ♣ 8 7                              ♣ A Q 9 6
                     S
                    ♠ 10 9 8
                    ♡ A K 7 5
                    ◊ A Q 5
                    ♣ 10 4 2
```

Four hearts doubled, making four. As we perused the hand record after the evening game, I couldn't help but mention board 11. Of course, I was thrilled with our second place overall finish, but we had lost the event to the flight A pair by a single matchpoint.

"Look at board 11," I said to partner. " What lousy luck. Are you telling me that's a random computer hand? That 22 point game is cold. Give me the king of clubs and East the king of diamonds, and they're down a bunch. We have two sixty per cent plus games and finish second. And, of course, if you hadn't bid four diamonds-"

" I know I shouldn't have bid again," partner said interrupting my raving, " but what did we get on the board?"

"Huh?"

"I said what did we get on the board?"

"We got a three."

"Imagine if you hadn't doubled."

That guy Zeno. Do you think he was a bridge player?

♠ ♡ ◇ ♣

C  H  A  P  T  E  R   3  7
# The Accident

*Keep cool. It will all be one a hundred years hence.*
- Ralph Waldo Emerson

Accidents will happen. That's a fact, albeit an unpleasant one, of
life at the bridge table. You misbid, you forget your system, you
over or underestimate your hand. You wind up in the wrong spot, and it
seems certain you're headed for a terrible board.

Keeping your cool when such a circumstance arises is important for
a number of reasons. First, you must keep a clear head and play the hand
as well as you can. You might think you're getting a bad board, but you do
not know the result until the hand is over and you look at the traveler.
Second, you never want to let your opponents know you're in trouble. If
they realize that something is amiss, they might find the killing switch before you have time to run with your tricks.

Finally, if the board does indeed turn out to be bad, it's only one
board. A zero is a zero is a zero. Next board. Bridge goes on, and you
can still have a decent game in spite of a bad result or two. As in golf,
where the most important shot in your round is the next one, the same is
true in bridge. The most important deal in the session is the one you are
about to play.

A case in point is this deal from a recent club game:

**DLR: NORTH   VUL: N-S**

```
                    ♠ A J 3
                    ♡ A 10 8 6 3
                    ◇ A J
                    ♣ Q 8 3

    ♠ 9 8 6 5            N            ♠ K Q 7 4
    ♡ Q 9 5 4                         ♡ K J 7
    ◇ 6 4 3        W  ✦  E            ◇ K 8 7 5
    ♣ 7 5                             ♣ A 9
                        S

                    ♠ 10 2
                    ♡ 2
                    ◇ Q 10 9 2
                    ♣ K J 10 6 4 2
```

Before the story goes on, can you guess what the final contract was in this hand? It was two spades by South- making two! Here's what happened. I was North and opened ONE NO TRUMP. I had a five card heart suit, but I had honors in the other suits and a balanced hand. East doubled. As you can see, I do quite well in ONE NO TRUMP doubled. My wife, Claudia, however, reasonably thought we would do better in clubs. Forgetting that in our system all transfers are off after interference, she bid TWO SPADES as a transfer to clubs. Everyone passed. Oops!

"Before you lead," Claudia told East, "my partner should have announced my bid was a transfer to clubs."

"We don't play transfers after interference," I said.

Oh boy, what had she gone and done now? This wasn't going to be pretty, and us vulnerable. I must admit I've been in situations like this and haven't handled them well.

I fuss and fume over the missed transfer and blow the hand. Not Claudia. She never batted an eyelash. She got a favorable heart lead and made the most of it. She took the ace and ruffed a heart. She then led a diamond to the ace (would I have taken the finesse?) and ruffed another heart.

She now led another diamond. East switched to the king of spades (too late), but at least she did make her contract. Disaster right? We could surely make four clubs. But look what happened. One pair got to clubs making 130. All other pairs apparently opened my hand ONE HEART. East overcalls ONE NO TRUMP. That goes down two for +100 for North-South. One pair was in two hearts by West(?) down two. All other pairs were in two spades by East, also down two. Only the side with the 5 card spade fit can make TWO SPADES. The side with the eight card fit goes down! Had Claudia gone down in TWO SPADES, we would have gotten a zero. Instead, her unflustered play got us a next to top.

Remember, when an accident happens, keep cool.

♠ ♡ ◇ ♣

PART FOUR
# Declarer Play

The play of the hand. This is what bridge players live for. Bidding and defense are partnership skills, something you must do in conjunction with someone else, but when *you* are the declarer, the spotlight is solely on *you*. *Your* partner puts down the dummy for *you* and plays out its cards at *your* command. The opponents scrutinize *your* line of play and try to counteract it. The kibitzers study *your* technique and marvel at *your* prowess with the cards.

Have *you* read your Watson and *your* Root? Are *you* ready? *Your* partner has accepted *your* invitation, perhaps taking into account *your* play of the cards, and put *you* into *your* game or *your* slam. It's where *you* wanted to be. *Your* LHO has tabled his opening lead, *your* partner has set down the dummy, and the spotlight has brightened and focused in. It's up to *you.*

It's time for a little showin' off.

Of course, if you are like me, your plans don't always turn out the way you had expected them to, and you have to be ready to dip into your finely honed arsenal of excuses.

Will somebody please turn down that spotlight?

# C H A P T E R   3 8
# Showin'off

*Egotism is the anesthetic that dulls the pain of stupidity.*
- Frank Leahy

Bridge players, like everyone else, have egos. Perhaps the only difference is that the average bridge ego is just a tad larger than normal. Who doesn't like to see his or her name at the top of the re-cap sheet or somewhere on the overall list? Who doesn't like to make that perfect bid or pull off some esoteric maneuver such as a three suited squeeze or a strip and endplay against the opponents? And who doesn't like to trump in at trick two with the ace of trumps just to show off the wonderful quality and depth of your trump suit? The only problem, though, is that the bridge ego can sometimes be the greatest obstacle to playing good bridge.

At a recent club game, I picked up: ♠: Q J 10 4 3 2  ♡: A 8 2  ◇: A ♣: 7 5 2

My wife, Claudia, sitting North, opened ONE CLUB. RHO, a renowned light bidder who loved to interfere with his opponents' auctions, overcalled TWO HEARTS. I bid TWO SPADES and Claudia jumped to FOUR SPADES. I fell in love with my six spades, my stiff ace of diamonds (not a good idea according to Mike Lawrence) and my Ace of hearts, so I went to Key Card Blackwood. Claudia showed three key cards, the other two aces and the king of trump. I bid FIVE NO TRUMP asking for kings, found that we were missing one and settled into SIX SPADES. Claudia, apparently having something of her own that she fell in love with and totally discounting my declarer play, bid SEVEN SPADES.

LHO led the 10 of hearts, and I waited with more than a little apprehension for the dummy. Here was the entire deal:

**DLR: NORTH   VUL: N-S**

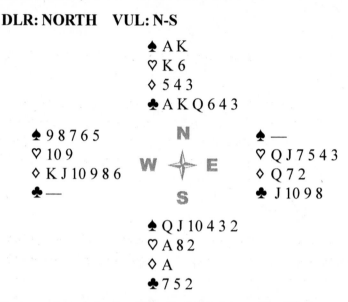

```
                    ♠ A K
                    ♡ K 6
                    ◇ 5 4 3
                    ♣ A K Q 6 4 3
  ♠ 9 8 7 6 5              N              ♠ —
  ♡ 10 9                                  ♡ Q J 7 5 4 3
  ◇ K J 10 9 8 6    W  ─┼─  E             ◇ Q 7 2
  ♣ —                      S              ♣ J 10 9 8
                    ♠ Q J 10 4 3 2
                    ♡ A 8 2
                    ◇ A
                    ♣ 7 5 2
```

So it was her clubs that Claudia fell in love with. Not very scientific bidding on our part, but the result seemed fine. What could go wrong? Everything, as I was about to learn. As Claudia has told me numerous times, this was a DISTRIBUTIONAL HAND. RHO's skip bid of TWO HEARTS was a warning sign. There would be some unusual DISTRIBUTION to contend with here. Without giving any of that a single thought, I flamboyantly called for the king of hearts at trick one just to show LHO what silly and useless bids his partner was wont to make. I didn't realize it at the time, but the hand was now doomed, at least with me at the helm.

I played the ace of spades and saw that LHO had the five outstanding trumps. Oh, oh. DISTRIBUTIONAL HAND. But I was still all right, wasn't I? As long as the clubs behaved, I still had thirteen tricks. Was there anything else? Could I ruff a heart with the king of spades? No, that would give LHO a spade trick. Oh well, what were the odds of the clubs splitting 4-0? Very good in this DISTRIBUTIONAL HAND.

I drew the remaining trumps, led a club to dummy, and that was the end of that. I could ruff the fourth club, but I couldn't get back to dummy. I had to lose a heart. Down one.

"Bad luck," I said to Claudia. "If either the spades or the clubs split, I make it."

"It was a DIS-"

"I know, I know," I said. Maybe you should have thought of that when you bid seven."

"And maybe you should have thought before you went up with the king of hearts at trick one," she said. "If you save that entry, you can ruff the fourth club and then come back to dummy with it for the last two clubs. What were you thinking when you went up with the king? You were just showing off, weren't you?"

"I-

"By the way," she continued before I could reply, "didn't you have a squeeze even after you were done showing off? Play your last trump and East has to pitch either a heart or a club."

"Squeeze?"

"If you had managed that, then you'd have really had something to show off about."

♠ ♡ ◇ ♣

# C H A P T E R   3 9
# A Bridge Player At Risk

*The simpler I keep things, the better I play*
- Nancy Lopez - LPGA Hall of Fame

In 1983, The National Commission on Education suggested that our nation was at risk and that our schools should get back to rigorously teaching the basics. According to the commission, a knowledge of these basics was the foundation of success for the after school years. Thus began the back to basics movement in education.

There are similar philosophies in sports. In the foreword to his golf book *Getting Back To Basics*, Tom Watson said, "Einstein had to learn to add and subtract before he developed the theory of relativity. A golfer has to learn to grip the club and set up to the ball before he can drive it far and straight. In science or golf, the basics are crucial."

The same can be said of bridge. Bridge players forget their basics and begin to misplay one hand after another. We have all learned the basics, of course. Many of us have read the excellent bridge primer WATSON'S (no relation to Tom) *Classic Book On The Play Of The Hand* which covers such fundamentals as The Power of Honors, Suit Establishment at No Trump, Ruffing Power, Trump Management at Suit Play, and Plays Postponing the Trump Lead. According to Watson, "no beginner or even average player can hope to make successful use of advanced techniques until he has mastered the elementals."

I would have done well to have gone back to my Watson and remembered all of this before the following deal came up at the club:

♠ J 10 9 8 6 5
♡ 7
◊ J 9 6 5
♣ K 4

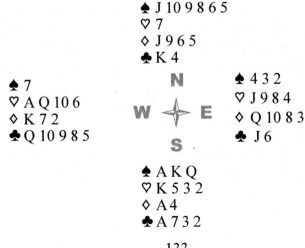

♠ A K Q
♡ K 5 3 2
◊ A 4
♣ A 7 3 2

I was South and opened 2NT. Claudia bid 3 HEARTS, a transfer to 3 SPADES, and she then put me in 4 SPADES. The opening lead was the 7 of spades. How would you play the hand? In spite of the fact that this contract is ice cold, I, forgot my Watson and went down.

Watson says to "form the habit of counting the number of tricks you are sure of making. If that falls short of your contract, count the number of tricks you have some expectation of making and then plan your play to make those tricks if possible."

There it was. I had nine tricks and a possible tenth if I led toward my heart king and the ace was on side. I drew trumps and led toward the king, a 50% chance. Alas, here was the entire deal:

**DLR: SOUTH    VUL: NONE**

♠ J 10 9 8 6 5
♡ 7
◊ J 9 6 5
♣ K 4

♠ 7
♡ A Q 10 6
◊ K 7 2
♣ Q 10 9 8 5

♠ 4 3 2
♡ J 9 8 4
◊ Q 10 8 3
♣ J 6

♠ A K Q
♡ K 5 3 2
◊ A 4
♣ A 7 3 2

Do you see the elementals from Watson that I did not consider- Ruffing Power and Plays Postponing the Trump Lead? Watson says that "Declarer, if he plays the hand at a suit contract, can eliminate the short suit from dummy and use dummy's trumps to ruff certain losers. Therefore, to make full use of dummy's small trumps, the declarer must keep them in dummy's hand."

I knew all of this, but I was blinded by the THREE HIGH TRUMPS in my hand which really had become the dummy as far as trumps were concerned. Ruffing hearts would get me no extra tricks because I would already make six trump tricks. I needed to eliminate diamonds, the short suit in my hand and ruff the rest with the ace and king of spades.

The trump lead would have held me to ten tricks. When East wins his diamond trick, he can lead a second trump. On any other lead, I can ruff two diamonds and make five. West didn't realize he had found a good lead which became a killing lead when declarer turned out to be a bridge player at risk.

"Not everyone bid game," Claudia said when she opened the traveler, "but they're all making four or five. What happened?"

"People must be leading the ace of hearts," I replied

"You wouldn't have that kind of luck, would you?" she said.

# CHAPTER 40

# Elementary, My Dear Watson

*Learn the fundamentals of the game and stick to them.*
- Jack Nicklaus

*Watson's Classic Book on the Play of the Hand at Bridge* is an excellent text for the advancing bridge player. The book takes you through all of the fundamentals of card play including finesses, entries, suit establishment, unblocking, trump management, and many more. The opening chapter of the book presents the principle upon which all of the succeeding chapters are based - "The Power of Honors." Watson stresses the importance of promoting the rank of lower cards as often as possible. "Whenever you win or attempt to win a trick, you should try to gain as many positions of rank as possible for your lower cards in the suit."

Good advice for an aspiring bridge player to remember. When my brother-in-law Eric and I first started playing duplicate together, I found a copy of Watson in a used book store and bought it for him as a gift. I told him that the lessons in the book, as elementary as they might seem, would be well worth remembering as he advanced through the world of bridge.

Several years later, I would have done well to remember those lessons myself when I was playing with Eric at the club and this hand came up:

**DLR: SOUTH    VUL: NONE**

```
                    ♠ A Q 7
                    ♡ A Q 10 8 7 4 3
                    ◊ Q
                    ♣ 8 2
    ♠ 10 4 3 2          N          ♠ K J 9
    ♡ 9                            ♡ 6 5
    ◊ 5 3 2       W  ✦  E          ◊ A K J 6 4
    ♣ K 9 7 6 5       S            ♣ Q J 10
                    ♠ 8 6 5
                    ♡ K J 2
                    ◊ 10 9 8 7
                    ♣ A 4 3
```

Eric was North. We play NAMYATS, so an opening bid of FOUR CLUBS tells partner to bid FOUR HEARTS, and an opening of FOUR DIAMONDS tells partner to bid FOUR SPADES.

The idea of NAMYATS is to expose the known hand and have the lead coming up to the unknown or closed hand. Often, that can save a trick. Eric opened the North hand FOUR CLUBS and I alerted. East overcalled FOUR DIAMONDS. Undaunted, I bid FOUR HEARTS and everyone passed. West led a diamond, East took the ace and shifted to the queen of clubs. Can you see how to make the hand without losing two spades, a diamond and a club? Good for you because I didn't.

I drew two rounds of trumps (too soon), led a diamond and pitched my second club from dummy (too late). East led another club and there was nothing I could do. Down one.

Eric opened the traveling score, and everyone else had made four hearts played from his direction!

"Come on," I said defensively to Eric. "If you're playing it, you would probably get a spade lead into your ace-queen."

"No," East said. " I'd never lead a spade from KJ9. I have a natural lead of the ace and king of diamonds. I don't see how you can make it when I switch to clubs."

"It's elementary," Eric said. "Promote the diamonds. Wasn't that in that Watson book you gave me?"

"I don't have the entries to use them," I whined.

"Not after you draw trump, you don't," Eric said. "At trick three lead your second diamond and pitch the club. You still have your two high trumps for entries. That was in Watson too, wasn't it? On your third diamond, pitch a spade. Your last diamond will be good, and you can throw the queen of spades on it. All you've lost are three diamond tricks, and now you have ten winners."

"But the spade finesse might have worked," I moaned.

"Sure," he needled me as brothers-in-law are wont to do. "Swap a 100% line of play for a 50% line. Those don't sound like very good odds to me. I thought the purpose of Namyats was for a possible overtrick, not an undertrick!"

Eric was right. My seven of diamonds was good as long as I used the queen, ten, nine and eight to promote it and preserved my king and jack of trumps in order to use it. Not a bad book, that Watson.

♠ ♡ ◇ ♣

# C H A P T E R     4 1
# Squeeze, Please!

*Please don't squeeze the Charmin.*
*- TV commercial*

Many bridge players think squeezes are in the realm of the game's esoterica. Squeezes are mysterious things that are done to us, not by us- things reserved for and understood by only the game's best players. Or, as is the case with the Vancelettes, they are things performed by accident in the fog of a migraine headache (See The Migraine Squeeze in Chapter 42).

This isn't necessarily so. According to Caroline Sydnor's BRIDGE MADE EASY, "Some squeezes are so easy Mr. Stumblebum could fall into the right play without realizing what he's doing."

Here's what to look for. Have you ever been in a contract and you see that you're one trick short? (Yes, you have, my wife Claudia would say to me...too many times.) This is when to look for a possible squeeze. Here is how Sydnor tells us to operate the squeeze.

1. You must be only one trick short of your contract.

2. You must surrender all but one of those tricks first. If you don't, the squeeze won't operate. Those esoteric players call this rectifying the count.

3. One defender must be busy protecting both suits in which you are hoping to find your extra trick. You must have an entry to each of your threat cards.

4. Now run your trumps. The last trump is the squeeze card. Many players clutch this last trump tight to their chests thinking they need it for protection. That's a mistake. It's the last trump that forces the fatal discard.

Here's how it worked for me at a recent sectional. I held : ♡: 10 9 8 7 6 4 3 ♠: A 9 6 ◊: 9 ♣: K 10. LHO opened THREE CLUBS, and my partner doubled. RHO passed, and I bid FOUR HEARTS. Here was the entire deal:

**DLR: WEST     VUL: N-S**

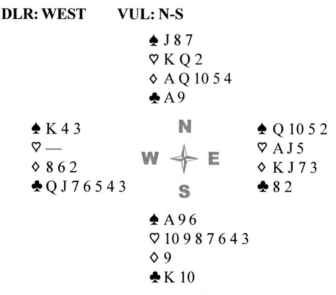

Oops! I had two heart losers, as I would soon find out, and two spade losers. I was one trick short. Hmmm. LHO led the club queen. I took the king and led a heart. RHO won and returned a club. I took the ace and played queen and another heart. RHO won and led a spade, kindly rectifying the count for me. I ducked and LHO won his king. He didn't realize it, but if he led a diamond now he would break up the squeeze. He returned a spade, however, to the 8, 10, and my ace.

If the diamond finesse worked, I would have ten tricks. Then I heard this little voice telling me no...the finesse can wait...run your hearts. So one after another, out they came, a parade of red out of my hand and onto the table. With three tricks to go, here was the ending:

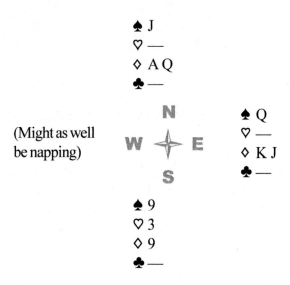

```
              ♠ J
              ♡ —
              ◊ A Q
              ♣ —

                    N              ♠ Q
(Might as well                     ♡ —
be napping)      W  ✛  E           ◊ K J
                    S              ♣ —

              ♠ 9
              ♡ 3
              ◊ 9
              ♣ —
```

I played my last heart and pitched the jack of spades from dummy. If you notice one of your opponents looking very uncomfortable, you know the squeeze is probably working. Maybe East's best play was to uncaringly pitch the jack of diamonds and let me guess. In reality, however, she pitched the queen of spades hoping in vain her partner held the nine. The nine of spades and the ace of diamonds were my last two tricks. At the other table, FOUR HEARTS was down one.

Yes, even Mr. Stumblebum can do it. So next time you're in what looks like a hopeless contract, lose those essential tricks first, then run your trumps. Good things might happen.

Happy squeezing!

♠ ♡ ◇ ♣

# CHAPTER 42
# The Migraine Squeeze

*In reality, serendipity accounts for one per cent of the
blessings we receive in life, work and love.
The other 99 per cent is due to our efforts.*
- Peter McWilliams

The word "serendipity" has an interesting origin. It comes to us from a Persian fairy tale in which the Three Princes of Serendip constantly made fortunate discoveries by accident. Bridge players are familiar with this experience if not, necessarily, with the word. Many of us simply stumble upon some of our great plays in a serendipitous manner. For the Vancelettes, one of those plays was the migraine squeeze.

At the time, we had been playing bridge for about seven years. We had accumulated enough points so that we were no longer ranked as novices, but neither of us had any pretensions about our abilities at the table. Our victories were still tempered by the number of gifts we received; any of our winning streaks inevitably turned into losing streaks; and misgivings about our ability to bid and play well wreaked havoc on our concentration. There was no doubt in our minds that we were still novices.

One criterion that we used to gauge our improvement was our ability to perform those bridge plays mastered only by the game's elite: the coup, the dummy reversal, the strip and endplay, and that mystery of mysteries, the squeeze. Oh, we could run a long suit and then all laugh when the opponents threw away the wrong card at trick twelve, but an actual squeeze with its rectifying of the count and its establishment of a threat card was still beyond us- well, beyond me, anyways. Claudia performed the feat at a regional tournament in Danvers, Massachusetts. I call it the migraine squeeze. It's the only kind of squeeze we knew.

We were playing in a flight C Swiss, and we were in and out of first place all day. By the break, Claudia had developed a migraine headache. While the rest of us went to dinner, she napped in the car hoping that she could hold together for three more rounds.

With one round to go, we were tied for second place. We sat down against a team of college students from the Boston area, and sitting North, I picked up: ♠: A107 ♡: 85 ◊: K652 ♣: A985. West opened ONE DIAMOND. I passed and East bid ONE SPADE. Claudia passed, and West bid TWO CLUBS. East bid a quiet TWO SPADES, and I thought that's where the bidding would end. But no. Suddenly Claudia emerged from her headache and bid THREE HEARTS! What was she doing? Where had she been on the first round of bidding? Had her headache obscured some points which she had just now discovered? West passed. I didn't want to miss game, so I bid THREE NO TRUMP. DOUBLE said West with enthusiasm. Again, Claudia emerged from her headache long enough to give me one of those "what have you done now, you idiot" looks. Then she bid FOUR HEARTS. There was a vociferous DOUBLE from West and another long look from Claudia, which ended the bidding.

Here was the entire deal:

**DLR: WEST      VUL: N-S**

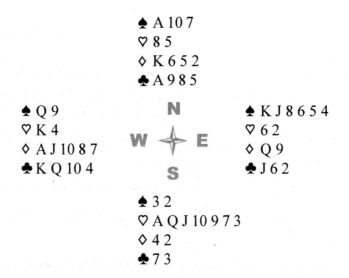

                 ♠ A 10 7
                 ♡ 8 5
                 ◊ K 6 5 2
                 ♣ A 9 8 5

♠ Q 9                        ♠ K J 8 6 5 4
♡ K 4                        ♡ 6 2
◊ A J 10 8 7                  ◊ Q 9
♣ K Q 10 4                   ♣ J 6 2

                 ♠ 3 2
                 ♡ A Q J 10 9 7 3
                 ◊ 4 2
                 ♣ 7 3

Oh no. What had I done? As you can see, Claudia has four tricks to lose. One in each suit. West led the king of clubs. Claudia took the ace and finessed a heart. West won, took his queen of clubs and led a third club that Claudia ruffed. Immediately she led a diamond toward the king. A light went on in my head. I had seen this in books! She was rectifying the count. She had four losers, but she was reducing the number to one.

West won his ace and returned a spade. Too late. Claudia took her ace of spades and ran her hearts. This was the three card ending:

```
              ♠ —
              ♡ —
              ◇ K 6
              ♣ 9
♠ —           N          ♠ K J
♡ —                      ♡ —
◇ J 10    W  ✦  E        ◇ Q
♣ 10          S          ♣ —
              ♠ 3
              ♡ A
              ◇ 4
              ♣ —
```

Without any visible fear, Claudia played her last heart, her ace, and West was squeezed. If he discarded a diamond, she could pitch the club on the board and her last two diamonds would be good. If West threw the club, then Claudia would pitch the diamond, and the King of diamonds and the 9 of clubs would take the last two tricks.

West pitched a diamond, Claudia pitched her club and led her last diamond to the dummy.

"Well done," said West dropping his last two cards in surrender.

"Yep," East said. "Too bad you didn't lead a spade earlier or the club when you were in last."

"I know. Right after I led the spade, I realized the squeeze was on."

"What are they talking about?" Claudia asked, breaking out of her headache's grip for one last time.

"You made it," I said. "The six of diamonds is good. You played it brilliantly."

"Three no trump was still a bozo bid," she said and then was lost to her pain for good, not even aware that we had won the event.

C H A P T E R    4 3

# Fear of Finessing - Part I

*Experience is what allows us to repeat*
*our mistakes, only with more finesse.*
- Derwood Fincher

All right, I admit it. My wife Claudia finally got me to acknowledge that I had Post Traumatic Finesse Syndrome and that I should go and see a finesse counselor. Not easy things for me to do.

"So," the counselor said as we began our session, "when did you first realize you had PTFS?"

It's not me," I demurred. "It's my wife."

"Your wife?"

"Yes. She has this phobia about taking finesses. One time, just once, she got an opening side suit lead through dummy's ace-queen. She finessed, East won and then made a killing switch. So that was it. Now Claudia refuses to take any finesses at all. I try telling her it's okay. Everyone in the room is taking that finesse, but no. She says the king might be singleton or the return might be fatal. So up she goes with her aces. No finesses for Claudia."

"Really? Then why are you here and not her?"

"Good question," I replied. "She's the one who fears finessing, not me. Can I go now?"

"Just one minute," the counselor said. "When your wife made the appointment for you..."

"Yes, yes, I know. The deal last month at the club."

"Right. And now she says that whenever you see a finessing situation your palms get all sweaty and your hands begin to tremble."

"It was just that one hand, I tell you. I do not have PTFS."

"So what was the deal?" asked the counselor.

I sketched it out for her on her pad:

**DLR: SOUTH    VUL: BOTH**

```
                    ♠ A 10 5 3
                    ♡ J 3
                    ◇ A 4 2
                    ♣ 10 9 8 6
   ♠ 8 4                N              ♠ K 9 7
   ♡ K 9 6                             ♡ 10 8 7 5 4
   ◇ J 7 6         W  ✦  E             ◇ 10 9 8 5
   ♣ Q 7 5 4 3                         ♣ 2
                       S
                    ♠ Q J 6 2
                    ♡ A Q 2
                    ◇ K Q 3
                    ♣ A K J
```

"I opened TWO NO TRUMP and wound up in FOUR SPADES. West led a diamond. I won my king and led the queen of spades. East won and returned that vicious little two of clubs. I finessed."

"I see," the counselor said sympathetically.

"West won and returned his highest club. East ruffed and dutifully led a heart. I needed this third finesse. Don't you see? I was going down if this one didn't work."

"You don't have to raise your voice," said the counselor.

"But I needed that heart finesse."

"You could afford to lose all three finesses and still make your game. What you could not afford was the ruff."

"You sound just like my wife. I'm not afraid to finesse, I tell you."

"You surely demonstrated that on this deal. That second finesse was an egregious error. A little warning bell should have gone off in your head when East led the club. Win the club and draw trumps. You still lose a club and a heart, but you'll make your game. Your wife was right. Again! That will be seventy-five dollars, please."

"But it was the TWO of clubs," I shouted. "The TWO!"

"Miss Snipple," the counselor called to her secretary in the other office, "get security in her please."

"But you have to listen to me..."

$$\spadesuit \ \heartsuit \ \diamondsuit \ \clubsuit$$

# CHAPTER 44
# Fear of Finessing - Part II

*Make up in finesse what you lack in force.*
- Jean Cocteau

"So you're back," said the finesse counselor with a knowing smile. "Your wife tells me you're at it again, taking every finesse in sight."

"They're fifty per cent chances," I said. "I like the odds."

"Then why all the symptoms of Post Traumatic Finesse Syndrome if you like those odds so much?"

"My finesses never work," I whined. "Whenever I make a bid that depends on a finesse, it won't work. It's just my luck."

"Ah yes," said the counselor. "Luck. Tell me about your luck."

I eagerly grabbed her pad and sketched out this deal from last week's game at the club:

**DLR: SOUTH     VUL: N-S**

```
                  ♠ A 6 5 4
                  ♡ 10 6 3 2
                  ♦ A 4 3
                  ♣ 7 5

  ♠ 7 2             N          ♠ Q J 10 9 3
  ♡ 7 5                        ♡ J
  ♦ Q J 10 9   W  ✦  E         ♦ 8 7 6
  ♣ K 6 4 3 2                  ♣ J 10 9 8
                    S
                  ♠ K 8
                  ♡ A K Q 9 8 4
                  ♦ K 5 2
                  ♣ A Q
```

"I was South," I said. "I opened two clubs and wound up in six hearts with the queen of diamonds lead."

"All very reasonable," said the counselor.

"Sure, except the club finesse lost and I wound up losing a diamond at the end."

"The club finesse," said the counselor, her voice rising. "You don't mean you took the club finesse?"

"That's what my wife said when I got home that night and showed her the hand. She smiled when I said yes, and then she made this appointment for me. I don't get it. What else is there to this hand besides the club finesse?"

The counselor sat shaking her head. "What did you get for a score on that board?" she inquired.

"A half. We tied one other unlucky pair. Five pairs didn't bid the slam. Can you imagine not being in slam with that hand?"

"It was a seven-table game then?"

"No," I answered hesitantly. "Eight."

"And who was at the eighth table?"

"Jim, our club's best player. He bid and made six. Talk about luck– I'll bet some little old lady led a club against him."

"Shame on you," scolded the counselor. "Jim got the same diamond lead that everyone else did. Your wife told me so on the phone. The hand is cold for six. Win the opening diamond lead in your hand and draw trumps. Now play the king and ace of spades and ruff a spade. West will show out on the third spade. Next cash the ace of diamonds and play your last diamond. West must win and either give you a ruff and sluff or lead into your club tenace. Only if East can win the diamond do you resort to taking the club finesse."

"But the finesse could have worked," I insisted. "It was a good bid, wasn't it?"

"I'm not so sure," said the counselor. "If you're going to keep taking every finesse in sight, maybe you should realize your limitations and just bid games."

"But I just made Life Master," I announced proudly.

"Hmmph. The way you butchered that hand, they should perhaps take points away from you. I hear there's a movement afoot to do just that in the ACBL. Not such a bad idea for some players maybe. That will be seventy-five dollars please."

♠ ♡ ◇ ♣

# The Finesse Counselor - A Return Visit

*Some people are so fond of ill luck that they*
*run half-way to meet it.*
*- Douglas William Jerrold*

It's nothing to worry about," the finesse counselor assured me. "Once you get Post Traumatic Finesse Syndrome, it tends to recur occasionally. It simply requires ongoing treatment."

"I'm telling you," I said emphatically, "I do not have PTFS."

"Your wife assures me she sees all the symptoms- the sweaty palms, the trembling cards whenever there's a finesse to be taken. And, of course, there's your tendency to take every finesse in sight- even the most illogical, the most absurd finesses."

"They're not absurd," I answered. "At duplicate, refusing to take a finesse can get you a bottom board."

"Yes," she countered, "and so can taking a finesse- like the one in the deal from the club last week that your wife told me about."

"That wasn't my fault."

She handed me her note pad. "Let's just see about that."

I wrote out the complete deal for her:

**DLR: SOUTH    VUL: E-W**

```
                    ♠ A K 9 8 6 5 3
                    ♡ 9 6 5
                    ◊ A 4
                    ♣ 3
    ♠ 10 7 2            N              ♠ Q
    ♡ Q 4 2                            ♡ 7 3
    ◊ K 3        W  ─┼─  E             ◊ Q J 10 9 8 7
    ♣ A Q 6 4 2         S              ♣ K 10 9 8
                    ♠ J 4
                    ♡ A K J 10 8
                    ◊ 6 5 2
                    ♣ J 7 5
```

"I was South and opened ONE HEART. West overcalled TWO CLUBS, and Claudia sitting North just jumped to FOUR HEARTS."

"Looks fine to me," said the counselor.

"What do you mean?" I grumbled. "Why didn't she bid her spades. The hand is cold for FOUR SPADES."

"It was good judgment for duplicate," she said. "The hand will make just ten tricks in spades when East leads the obvious high diamond, but it's cold for eleven tricks in hearts. All your losers can be pitched on the spades."

"Not on the defense I got," I moaned. "West led a spade. Where did he find that lead?"

"That seems perfectly logical to me unless you want him to lead from his ace-queen of clubs, his king of diamonds, or his queen of trumps. And the hand is still cold for eleven tricks on a spade lead, but your wife says you went down one. How in the world did you manage that?

"I took the ace of spades and led the nine of hearts of dummy."

"The nine?"

"Yes, the nine. For the finesse," I said impatiently. "Isn't that part of any bridge player's basic training? You lead the high card so you're still in dummy to repeat the finesse when it works."

"I'm afraid," said the counselor, "that in this case the only dummy was the one playing the hand."

"What do you mean?"

"Just tell me what happened."

"Bad luck. My finesses never work. West won, cashed his ace of clubs and then gave East a spade ruff. East led back his queen of diamonds, and I could get rid of only one of my losing diamonds. Down one."

"What's luck got to do, got to do with it?" the counselor chanted in her best Tina Turner voice. "You got exactly what you deserved on this hand. Didn't you see the queen of spades fall at trick one?"

"It could have been a false card from queen doubleton."

"Yes," said the counselor with a sigh, "I suppose it could have. But what if it wasn't? You should have asked yourself what might happen if your finesse lost. Disaster. You don't take a finesse when there's the danger of a ruff. Play the ace and king of hearts. When the queen doesn't fall, play the jack of spades, the ace of diamonds, and then run spades, pitching diamonds until West ruffs. He can take his ace of clubs, but that's it. Making five."

"But this was duplicate," I shouted. "If that finesse had worked, I would have taken all the tricks."

"You'd better keep it down or I'll have to get security in here again."

"Wait. You have to listen to me. It was duplicate. That's why I took that finesse. If it worked, I would have taken thirteen tricks. Don't you see?"

"Miss Snipple!"

# CHAPTER 46
# Don't Be Late

*It is cruel to discover one's mediocrity only when it is too late.*
- W. Somerset Maugham

My grandson Tyler's favorite nursery rhyme is the buckle your shoe verse which, in its fourth stanza, offers the advice "Don't be late." According to my wife Claudia, I should heed that simple maxim at the bridge table.

Here was a hand from a recent club game where my tardiness cost me dearly:

**DLR: SOUTH    VUL: N-S**

```
                    ♠ K 7 4
                    ♡ K J 5 4 3
                    ◇ K 2
                    ♣ Q 9 3

    ♠ 9 2              N              ♠ A 8 3
    ♡ A 7 6                           ♡ Q 9 8 2
    ◇ A 9 8 6      W  ✦  E            ◇ J 10 7 5 4
    ♣ J 10 6 5         S              ♣ 2

                    ♠ Q J 10 6 5
                    ♡ 10
                    ◇ Q 3
                    ♣ A K 8 7 4
```

I was in FOUR SPADES and got the jack of clubs lead. I had several chances for ten tricks if I could pick up the clubs, and maybe eleven if they ducked their ace of hearts. What could go wrong? Thoughtlessly, I led a spade at trick two. East took the ace and returned a low diamond. West won and led another club, which East ruffed. I won the diamond return and drew trumps. Of course, West took the setting trick when I led the ten of hearts.

"Lead the heart early," Claudia said. West might not take his ace if you do it at trick two."

"You would, wouldn't you?" I asked West imploringly.

"Probably not if you did it early," West said.

Claudia gave me her patented "I told you so" look, and I wanted to say to West- "Why not? Why wouldn't you be suspicious and grab that ace? I have no good discard to take on the king of hearts. Why should early make a difference?"

Second verse- worse than the first:

We were babysitting our grandson, and I was telling Claudia about a hand from the previous night at the club. I drew it out for her on a pad of paper.

**DLR: SOUTH    VUL: BOTH**

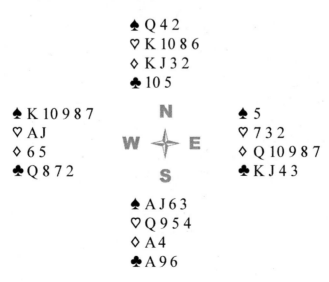

```
                    ♠ Q 4 2
                    ♡ K 10 8 6
                    ◇ K J 3 2
                    ♣ 10 5
  ♠ K 10 9 8 7          N          ♠ 5
  ♡ A J                            ♡ 7 3 2
  ◇ 6 5          W ✦ E            ◇ Q 10 9 8 7
  ♣ Q 8 7 2          S            ♣ K J 4 3
                    ♠ A J 6 3
                    ♡ Q 9 5 4
                    ◇ A 4
                    ♣ A 9 6
```

"I was South and in FOUR HEARTS. West led a club. East put up the jack, and I ducked."

"Why?"

"To cut their communication."

"I see," Claudia said.

"East switched to the five of spades. No matter what I did then, the opponents would score a club, a spade, the ace of trumps, and a spade ruff. But," I added proudly, "if I hadn't cut their communication, East could have led a club back to West for another spade ruff, and I would have gone down two."

"What if you take the ace of clubs early and get the hearts going right away?" Claudia asked. "Do you think they would have found their spade ruff then?"

"West could have taken the ace and led another club," I said. "Now East returns his singleton spade."

"You take the ace of spades and finish drawing trumps. What happened at the other tables?"

"It was the second time it had been played," I admitted. "At the other table, they made FOUR HEARTS."

"So take the ace of clubs early," Claudia said. "Don't give them a chance to find their best defense. Right Tyler? You tell him. Seven, eight..."

"Don't be late, Grandpa."

# C H A P T E R   4 7
# The Little Trump
# That Could

*Sometimes the small stuff is much more important than it looks.*
- Dale E. Lehman

Do you remember my favorite children's story, "The Little Engine That Could?"

In it, a little locomotive hauls a load of toys over a mountain when a bigger, incapacitated engine can not do it. Repeating, "I think I can, I think I can" to himself, the little engine completes the daunting task.

In bridge, we should save our littlest trump for the same sort of important job. In some deals, your littlest trump can be the most valuable card in your hand.

Bernard Magee made exactly that point in one of his August 1999 hands from *The Bridge Calendar*. The calendar is an excellent way to read one entertaining and informative bridge hand every day of the year. In this particular hand, Magee's trump suit was spades, and the side suit in dummy which he needed to set up was diamonds.

| | |
|---|---|
| ♠: AJ8763 | ♠: K42 |
| ◇: Q5 | ◇: AK874 |
| ♣: A74 | ♣: 963 |

The contract was FIVE SPADES. The opponents had cashed two hearts and now switched to a club. Declarer won his ace and was faced with getting rid of two losing clubs. He played the ace and king of spades, discovering the 2-2 split. Now came the queen, king and ace of diamonds, pitching one club. Diamonds split 4-2 and declarer ruffed the fourth diamond. But here is the key play. He must not ruff with the three of spades, his littlest trump. He ruffs with the six, and the three is then the little engine that can take him back to the four of spades in dummy, his only entry to the fifth diamond.

Says Magee, "Always value your lowest trump."

A valuable lesson, but one that came two weeks too late on my calendar. I was South in the following deal at our club, and my wife Claudia was North:

**VUL: E-W**       **DLR: EAST**

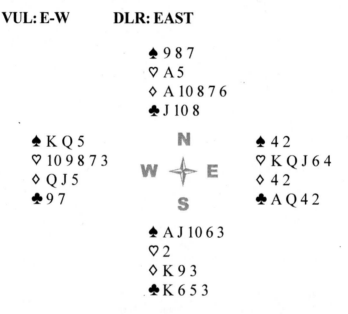

```
                    ♠ 9 8 7
                    ♡ A 5
                    ◊ A 10 8 7 6
                    ♣ J 10 8

    ♠ K Q 5              N           ♠ 4 2
    ♡ 10 9 8 7 3                     ♡ K Q J 6 4
    ◊ Q J 5          W   +   E       ◊ 4 2
    ♣ 9 7                            ♣ A Q 4 2
                         S
                    ♠ A J 10 6 3
                    ♡ 2
                    ◊ K 9 3
                    ♣ K 6 5 3
```

After East opened ONE HEART, I wound up in FOUR SPADES DOUBLED. West led the ten of hearts. I took the ace and led the nine of spades from dummy on which I played the <u>three</u>. East won the queen of spades and made the unfortunate switch to the queen of diamonds. Oh my! It looked like I was going to make this hand. I won with the king in my hand and played the ace of spades, both following. All I had to do now was play diamonds until someone ruffed and I was home.

West ruffed the fourth diamond and led a heart. Do you see what I did? Carelessly, I ruffed with the six of spades. As soon as it hit the table, I stared at the 8 of spades in dummy and the J 10 of spades in my hand. My little engine, my valuable little trump was sitting on the table in front of me. I had no way to that priceless fifth diamond in dummy and to the clubs so I could lead toward my king. I had turned +590 and a top to –100 and a zero.

"Locked yourself in your hand again, huh?" Claudia said when she saw the stunned look on my face and my inability to play to the next trick.

Remember, your littlest trump can be the most valuable card in your hand. Use it wisely.

♠ ♡ ◇ ♣

# C H A P T E R  4 8
# The Thinker

*Beware when the Great God lets loose a thinker on the planet.*
- Ralph Waldo Emerson

Bridge is a game for thinkers. Every hand is a problem to be solved, a puzzle to be figured out. It is a game where you can use both logic and intuition to work out the opponents' distribution and even the location of a particular card. Constructive thinking at the bridge table breeds success.

With all of that said, it must also be stated that there are times in bridge when you can think too much. This can result in overplaying the hand, losing tricks that you would not have lost had you played in a straightforward manner.

Look what happened with this deal at a recent club game. Two sweet little old ladies, arguably the most fearsome foes in bridge, came to our table, and we picked up the following cards:

**DLR: NORTH   VUL: N-S**

```
                    ♠ J 9
                    ♡ K Q 7
                    ◇ K 10 4 2
                    ♣ A 10 9 8

   ♠ 5 3 2             N            ♠ A 10 6 4
   ♡ J 9 8                          ♡ 5 3 2
   ◇ A            W  ✦  E           ◇ Q J 7 6 3
   ♣ K J 7 6 5 4        S           ♣ Q

                    ♠ K Q 8 7
                    ♡ A 10 6 4
                    ◇ 9 8 5
                    ♣ 3 2
```

This is the kind of hand that Kay, Silodor and Karpin talk about in THE COMPLETE BOOK OF DUPLICATE BRIDGE in their chapter called "The Fight for the Partial." More than 50% of all deals are properly played at a partscore contract, and it is in this life or death struggle for the partscore where one achieves success or suffers failure at matchpoints.

Claudia, North, opened ONE DIAMOND, and I, South, responded ONE HEART.

Claudia with her king, queen third of hearts bid TWO HEARTS, and that ended the auction. The two ladies (let's call them Martha and Pearl) were politely quiet during the bidding.

Martha, sitting West, led her stiff ace of diamonds. Pearl, seeing the king in dummy, played her 7 of diamonds asking for a spade, Martha complied, and Pearl won the ace of spades. Instead of returning a diamond, however, Pearl led what I didn't realize was her stiff queen of clubs.

I could now make three by winning this and drawing trumps. I saw no reason, though, to win the first club. Pearl was momentarily stunned when her club held, but she recovered quickly and led a diamond. The play now was excruciating: diamond ruff, club ruff, diamond ruff. Down one! At all other tables they made two or three hearts.

As is the case with all such results, there was much conversation at the table as I wrote down the score.

"Nice play," said Martha.

"I know," said Pearl. "I couldn't believe it when my club won. I probably should have just given you your diamond ruff."

"Oh no," Martha said. "You did just fine."

"Why did you duck the club?" Claudia couldn't resist asking.

"I was cutting their communication."

"Gosh," she said, "it seems to me they communicated just fine."

# C H A P T E R     4 9
# Safety First

*The only safe course for the defeated is to expect no safety.*
- Virgil

Ah, the safety play. Sounds reassuring, doesn't it? In the hazardous realm of declarer play fraught with bad splits and offside singleton kings, there is the comforting existence of a play that is a form of insurance against all of this.

According to Terrence Reese in *Blocking, Unblocking, & Safety Plays In Bridge*, "When you are playing a contract that seems to be laydown, pause and say to yourself 'can I lose this contract if the breaks are extremely bad?' If the answer is yes, then look for a safety play." If, for instance, your trump suit is:

Q J 7 2

A 9 4 3

the safety play is to enter the hand and lead a low trump towards dummy. That way, if West holds K1085, he only makes one trick.

In duplicate, however, the overtrick can be worth as much as the contract itself. If East in the above situation holds K85, the "safety play" would unnecessarily lose to the king and give poor declarer a zero. According to Kay, Silodor and Karpin in *The Complete Book Of Duplicate Bridge* "at matchpoint play one cannot adopt as his guiding philosophy the approach of playing for 'safety.' If one does, he is wasting his talents and must inevitably be a loser."

I would have done well to heed this advice at the club recently when, playing with my wife Claudia, I picked up in 4th position: ♠: A Q 3  ♡: K  ◇: A Q J 10 7 3  ♣: 8 6 5 I hate hands like this. I never know how much to value my stiff king. Do I have 13 or 16 points? What do I rebid when I open ONE DIAMOND and partner responds ONE HEART? What if she responds ONE SPADE? Actually it's a little easier if partner is a passed hand. I would then tend to bid more conservatively.

While I was filtering all of this information through my muddled bridge mind, everyone else at the table was busy making bids. LHO opened THREE HEARTS. Now what would I bid? But wait. Claudia reached into her bid box and placed a DOUBLE card on the table. Wow! She had to have some diamonds for her double. But what about spades? She must have those too. How could I show my hand? Enough. I reached into my bid box, placed the SIX DIAMONDS card on the table and waited with trepidation for the dummy to come down. The opening lead was the queen of hearts! Here was Claudia's hand: ♠: K J 5 2 ♡: A 3 ◊: 9 6 2 ♣: A K 4 3 Holy bridge gods! The hand was cold. I won the trick with my stiff king. My losing club would go on the ace of hearts. At most I would lose a diamond if the king was offside. Then, a dangerous thing happened. I began to think. I'd have to get to dummy to finesse diamonds. What if West was void in either clubs or spades and ruffed? Now I wouldn't know whether to take the diamond finesse. So...Safety Play! I plunked down the ace of diamonds. It would add insult to injury if LHO held the stiff king. After all, I had one. Alas, here was the entire hand:

**DLR: WEST     VUL: NONE**

```
                    ♠ K J 5 2
                    ♡ A 3
                    ◊ 9 6 2
                    ♣ A K 4 3

  ♠ 4                  N              ♠ 10 9 8 7 6
  ♡ Q J 7 6 5 4 2                     ♡ 10 9 8
  ◊ 8 4          W  ✦  E              ◊ K 5
  ♣ Q J 2                             ♣ 10 9 7
                     S
                    ♠ A Q 3
                    ♡ K
                    ◊ A Q J 10 7 3
                    ♣ 8 6 5
```

163

Oh well. I forced out the king of diamonds and claimed–making six. Claudia opened the traveling score and unbelievably everyone had bid the slam, taken the finesse and made seven except for one table. There East-West had sacrificed in SIX HEARTS and gone down 1400! My thoughtful play had gotten us a zero.

"What were you doing? Claudia asked.

"Safety play," I explained.

"Gee," she said, "I have so much to learn about this game."

C  H  A  P  T  E  R      5  0
# Thin Ice

*"In skating over thin ice, our safety is in our speed."*
- Ralph Waldo Emerson

In the previous chapter, I told you about an ill-conceived safety play that I made. Forgetting that it is best not to adopt a philosophy of safety when playing duplicate bridge, I eschewed an obvious finesse in a slam and plunked down my ace of trumps in the hopes of dropping a stiff king. Instead, I got us a zero when the rest of the field took the finesse and made an overtrick. Safety plays are for imps. Not wimps, IMPS, when overtricks are meaningless and making your contract should be your main concern. Right? Right.

So why didn't I remember my own advice when I played in a recent sectional Swiss Teams with my partner, Bob Rosenberg? In first seat, I picked up:

♠: A Q 10   ♡: 8 5   ◇: K J 7 6 5   ♣: A 9 2

I opened 1 Diamond. LHO overcalled 1 Spade. Bob said 2 Hearts. RHO passed, and I bid 2NT. LHO now bid 3 Clubs, and Bob bid 3 Spades. What was that? I had already informed him of my spade stopper, but I guess he wanted to know again, so I bid 3NT. Everyone passed, LHO led the 8 of clubs, and Bob tabled this dummy:

♠: 9 8 7   ♡: A K Q 9 7 4 3   ◇: 10   ♣: J 4

I was dumbfounded. Why weren't we in hearts? Surely hearts would be safer and make more tricks. I called for dummy's jack, and it held. Whew! Of course, I would have known that for sure if I had applied the rule of 11. Still mesmerized by that long string of hearts and not giving a single thought to the thin ice upon which I was skating, I hastily called for the ace of hearts. Hand over! Down one. Alas, Emerson's advice might be good for the ice, but not for the bridge table. Here was the entire, incredible deal:

**DLR: SOUTH    VUL: N-S**

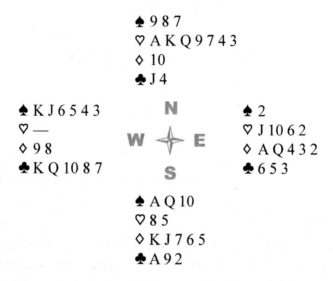

```
                    ♠ 9 8 7
                    ♡ A K Q 9 7 4 3
                    ◇ 10
                    ♣ J 4

♠ K J 6 5 4 3            N            ♠ 2
♡ —                                   ♡ J 10 6 2
◇ 9 8          W  ✦  E                ◇ A Q 4 3 2
♣ K Q 10 8 7            S             ♣ 6 5 3

                    ♠ A Q 10
                    ♡ 8 5
                    ◇ K J 7 6 5
                    ♣ A 9 2
```

When my jack of clubs held, all I had to do was stop and ask myself what could go wrong with what appeared to be a cold contract. It didn't matter whether we were in hearts or no trump. Making my vulnerable game should have been priority one. A 4-0 heart split was the only thing that could send me plunging into the cold oblivion of down one. I could have insured my contract against this possibility, which had been suggested in the bidding, by leading a low heart from dummy at trick two. The opponents could have done nothing to hurt me, and the contract would have been safe. Incredibly, 4 Hearts has no play in this hand, and Bob was right to leave me in 3NT.

The story is not over, however. It seldom is in bridge. At the other table (you never know what's happening there) our teammates were in 5 Clubs doubled, a phantom sacrifice over a 4 heart bid, down 1100. My play made no difference except that we lost the match by 4 more imps. I still wish I had made the right play. Win or lose, you like to play good bridge. Of course, if our teammates had set four hearts and I had made 3 no trump...

♠ ♡ ◇ ♣

# C H A P T E R   5 1
# A Little Help

*I get by with a little help from my friends.*
- John Lennon & Paul McCartney

Bridge is a highly competitive sport, but it is played in an environment of propriety and good sportsmanship. Like golfers, bridge players practice active ethics and have zero tolerance for boorish behavior. Your opponents are your friends.

None of this, however, precludes you from using your friends to help you make your contracts. In fact, there are times when you simply can not get by in bridge without a little help from your friends.

Observe this hand from a recent club game:

**VUL: N-S          DLR: WEST**

```
                    ♠ A 6 5 3
                    ♡ A Q 5 4
                    ◇ 5
                    ♣ K 7 6 5

   ♠ K Q J 10         N          ♠ 9 7 4
   ♡ K 8                         ♡ 10 9 3 2
   ◇ K J 8 7      W  ✦  E        ◇ 9 6 3 2
   ♣ Q 10 9         S            ♣ 8 4

                    ♠ 8 2
                    ♡ J 7 6
                    ◇ A Q 10 4
                    ♣ A J 3 2
```

167

I was South. My brother-in-law, Eric, was West and opened the hand ONE DIAMOND. My wife, Claudia, doubled. I decided to shoot out THREE NO TRUMP. Eric led the king of spades. Hmmm. I had five top tricks. How would you play the hand? I figured I needed Eric to lead suits for me, so I led back a spade at trick two. After Eric enjoyed his spades, he had to give me a trick. He made the best return of the king of hearts (he's always so unwilling to help). After three rounds of hearts, I noted that Eric was down to clubs and diamonds. Now I could force him to help me one more time. I played the ace, king and another club. Eric was in and had to lead a diamond. I made 3 clubs, 3 hearts, 2 diamonds and a spade. Three no trump bid and made was a top. Notice that if I do either clubs or diamonds at trick two, I will lose 3 spades, a diamond and a club.

Then, at a recent sectional:

**VUL: N-S       DLR: SOUTH**

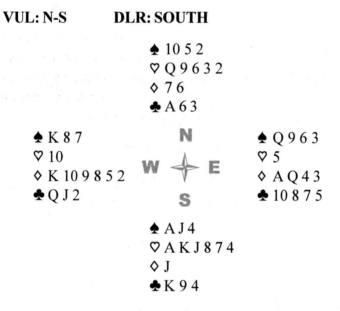

```
                    ♠ 10 5 2
                    ♡ Q 9 6 3 2
                    ♢ 7 6
                    ♣ A 6 3
 ♠ K 8 7                              ♠ Q 9 6 3
 ♡ 10                 N               ♡ 5
 ♢ K 10 9 8 5 2   W ⟡ E               ♢ A Q 4 3
 ♣ Q J 2             S                ♣ 10 8 7 5
                    ♠ A J 4
                    ♡ A K J 8 7 4
                    ♢ J
                    ♣ K 9 4
```

I was South and opened ONE HEART. Claudia jumped to FOUR HEARTS with the North hand. West led the 8 of diamonds. East won and, refusing to give me any help at all, switched to a trump. Oops! I only had nine top tricks. How could I make four hearts?

I looked at the spades. What about a finesse? No. As much as I loved finesses, there was no finesse here. If I led the spade ten, East would cover (wouldn't he?), and I'd have to play my ace. If I had the nine of spades, then I would have a legitimate double finesse in spades. The only way I could succeed now, however, was if East had both spade honors and I could later lead toward my jack.

But wait. This hand was cold no matter where the spade honors were. All I needed was a little help from my friends. If I could induce them to lead spades, I would make two spade tricks- and my contract.

First I ruffed dummy's remaining diamond. Then I played the ace, king, and a third club. No matter which opponent won, they would have to lead spades. If they led a diamond or a club, I would get a ruff-sluff (ruff in one hand, pitch a spade from the other) and only lose a diamond, a club, and a spade. If I didn't ruff the diamond first, the opponent who won the club could exit with a diamond, and I would have to lead spades myself.

West won the club and led a spade. I played low from dummy, captured East's queen with my ace, conceded one more spade trick, and claimed. Bidding and making four hearts was worth a 9 ½ on an 11 top. Some pairs did not bid the game, and some, alas, must have tried for the non-existent spade finesse and gone down one.

"Nicely played," said my right hand opponent.

"Yes, well done," said my left hand opponent.

It was easy. All I needed was a little help from my friends.

C H A P T E R  5 2
# Not Norm

*When they don't cover, they don't have it."*
- Zia Mahmood's winning 1989 Bols Bridge Tip

Good advice from Zia. So many players have learned and swear by the axiom "cover an honor with an honor," that they almost stop thinking constructively at the bridge table. Toss out an honor or call for one from dummy and they will cover it with a higher honor if they have it. If they don't cover, it is almost a certainty that they don't have it.

This advice is particularly valuable when you are faced with a two-way finesse. Here's a hand that I played from a recent sectional:

**DLR: WEST     VUL: BOTH**

```
                    ♠ Q J 6
                    ♡ Q 8 7
                    ◇ Q J 8 7
                    ♣ 9 5 3

  ♠ K 2                 N            ♠ 9 3
  ♡ A 6 5 2                          ♡ K J 10 3
  ◇ 5 3          W  ✦  E             ◇ K 10 6 2
  ♣ K Q J 10 7          S            ♣ 6 4 2

                    ♠ A 10 8 7 5 4
                    ♡ 9 4
                    ◇ A 9 4
                    ♣ A 8
```

I was East declaring a contract of 3 HEARTS after South had over-called in Spades. South led the ace of clubs. Then, thinking he had made an unfortunate lead, played his ace of spades and then his ace of diamonds and another. Nine tricks were now assured, but where was the queen of trumps? True, no other East probably had the luxury of being in his hand at trick four, but could I take advantage of it? I led the jack of hearts, and South played low without a thought. So I went up with the ace and finessed the ten on the way back. Making 170 was worth an 11 on a 12 top. If they don't cover it, they don't have it, right? Thanks Zia. But wait, not so fast. Observe this hand from the club several weeks later:

**DLR: SOUTH    VUL: NONE**

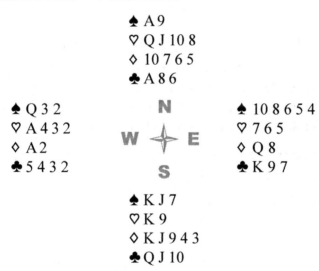

```
                    ♠ A 9
                    ♡ Q J 10 8
                    ♦ 10 7 6 5
                    ♣ A 8 6

     ♠ Q 3 2              N            ♠ 10 8 6 5 4
     ♡ A 4 3 2                         ♡ 7 6 5
     ♦ A 2          W  ──  E           ♦ Q 8
     ♣ 5 4 3 2                         ♣ K 9 7
                         S
                    ♠ K J 7
                    ♡ K 9
                    ♦ K J 9 4 3
                    ♣ Q J 10
```

I was declaring 3 N T with the South hand against a couple from our club, Norm and Marsha. Marsha, sitting West, led a diabolical club. How much easier my life would have been if she had led a heart! East won the king and returned a club. I had to knock out the ace of diamonds and the ace of hearts. I won the club in dummy and played the 10 of diamonds. Norm, sitting East, dropped the 8 without any thought. Hmm. If the queen of diamonds was on my left and the ace on my right, I could lose two diamonds, a club, and a heart. And, for all that Norm knew, Marsha could have three diamonds to the A-9, and he would be costing his side a trick by not covering if he had the queen. So, cleverly, I went up

171

with the king of diamonds. Down one. I lost two clubs, two diamonds, and a heart. Everyone else made three and four.

"What were you doing?" my wife Claudia asked me.

"Zia said if they don't cover it, they don't have it." I said.

"That's Zia," said Claudia, "not Norm."

# C H A P T E R  5 3
# Duck

*For all we have and are*
*For all our children's fate*
*Stand up and take the war*
*The Hun is at the gate!*
- Rudyard Kipling

Stand...stand up and you be a man!
- William Shakespeare

Good advice from Kipling and Shakespeare. Good, that is, for the soldier about to defend the realm or the young Romeo, who must stand tall for his lady Juliet. Not so good, however, for the bridge player. More often than not, the bridge player would be better served to heed a more prudent albeit far less romantic bit of advice- duck!

I could have used that advice at our club, not once but twice when a new couple arrived shortly before game time. When they got to our table, they introduced themselves as Les and Marion.

"Les and Marion," I said. "Those were my parents' names."

"Really," said Marion. "How nice."

They seemed like a pleasant, innocuous couple, but their appearance and their names belied the havoc they were about to wreak upon my partner and me. This was our first board:

173

**DLR: SOUTH    VUL: N-S**

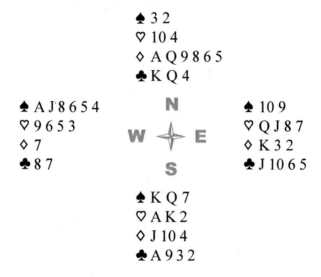

                    ♠ 3 2
                    ♡ 10 4
                    ◊ A Q 9 8 6 5
                    ♣ K Q 4

♠ A J 8 6 5 4                          ♠ 10 9
♡ 9 6 5 3                              ♡ Q J 8 7
◊ 7                                    ◊ K 3 2
♣ 8 7                                  ♣ J 10 6 5

                    ♠ K Q 7
                    ♡ A K 2
                    ◊ J 10 4
                    ♣ A 9 3 2

I was South and opened 1NT. My partner raised me to game. Les, sitting West, led the five of spades, and Marion played the nine. If the diamond finesse was on, I could see 12 tricks.

Yes, yes, I know all about ducking plays, but those were when you held three to the ace, weren't they? (No.) Furthermore, it wasn't right, was it, to duck in duplicate where overtricks were so important? As you can see, I should have ducked. Marion's nine would win the first trick. When she returned the ten, I would perforce cover and Les would have to win his ace-or lose it. I would lose two spades and a diamond but score 10 tricks and plus 630.

Dazzled by the prospect of 12 tricks, however, I won my spade queen and led the jack of diamonds. Marion ducked. I don't know why she ducked. They could have beaten me two tricks at that point, but perhaps Marion wasn't sure of the spade position, or perhaps she thought Les was beginning a high-low signal with the seven of diamonds, so she had to duck to cut me off from dummy.

At any rate, Les showed out on the second diamond. I turned to clubs. They didn't break, and I lost the last five tricks. Not so nice, I thought, for people named Les and Marion.

Les and Marion were back the following week. I made a joke about remembering to duck against them, and we began to play.

```
              ♠ Q 8
              ♡ A 3
              ◊ A J 8 6 5 4 3
              ♣ 4 2

                    N

              W  ✦  E

                    S

              ♠ K 9 3
              ♡ K Q 4 2
              ◊ Q 7
              ♣ A Q 5 3
```

I opened 1NT, and my partner raised me to game. Les, again sitting West, led the jack of spades.

All those lovely diamonds in dummy and a spade lead from Les. A sense of deja vu all over again gnawed at me. But no. Les couldn't get me this time. With the ace on my right, I could hold up my king and then play on diamonds.

I didn't recognize the only possible danger in this layout- six spades to the A-J-10 in the West hand- nor did I see the need for another ducking play. I played the queen of spades and it held. Oh, oh. Timorously, I came to my hand with a heart and led the queen of diamonds. Marion took her king and led her remaining spade through my king. When Les finished cashing his five spade winners, I was down two.

The moral: if you ever encounter two bridge players with your parents' names, don't forget that most important bridge maxim of all- duck!

♠ ♡ ◇ ♣

# CHAPTER 54
# The Fine Art of Balancing

*Don't forget to count*
- The Count from Sesame Street

I have a confession to make. I don't count! Oh, I count trumps when I'm drawing them, but I have been known to botch even that.

"I have the rest," I'll say, making a claim.

"Lead a diamond, please," one of my opponents will say to his partner.

No problem. All of my diamonds are good. But then the opponent produces the last trump that I forgot to draw.

What I'm talking about, though, is counting out the hand, drawing inferences from the bidding and the play to figure out the opponents' distribution. I can even remember, when my wife Claudia and I learned the game with our friends David and Mary, we kept little notepads on the table and wrote down an opponent's distribution when we thought we had it figured out. "Three hearts," one of us would open, and the rest of us would grab our pencils.

We knew this was an important skill to master. As David Bird said in his review of *Countdown To Winning Bridge*, an excellent book on the subject by Tim Bourke and Marc Smith, "if you have been playing bridge without counting the hand, perhaps for many years, you are about to enter a new world." And H.W. Kelsey in *Killing Defence At Bridge* said, "Why is it then that so many intelligent adults produce the wrong count at the table? Mostly it is a matter of mental laziness. You know very well that you ought to count, but when partner shows out on the second round of trumps, you merely register hazily that declarer must have quite a lot without making the effort to work out just how many."

That was me. I had never entered David Bird's new world of counting, and I had been mentally lazy until one night at the club when this deal came along, a little light went on, and I finally got it. I was South and picked up:

♠: Q J 8 3 ♡: 4 ◊: J 9 2 ♣: A J 9 7 4. West opened a weak TWO HEARTS. My wife Claudia doubled, and East bid THREE HEARTS. I bid THREE SPADES, and Claudia raised me to FOUR SPADES. West led the heart king and I saw:

| South (me) | Dummy |
|---|---|
| ♠ Q J 8 3 | ♠ A 10 6 |
| ♡ 4 | ♡ A J |
| ◊ J 9 2 | ◊ K Q 7 4 |
| ♣ A J 9 7 4 | ♣ K 10 8 5 |

Hmm. Another Moisian (4-3) trump fit. How did I always manage to find those? Anyways, how could I make this contract? I'd need to find trumps 3-3, knock out the ace of diamonds, and then I would need to find the club queen. I never get those two-way finesses right.

I took the ace of hearts, and the played the ace and another spade. East helped me by taking his king and returning a spade, all following. I now led a diamond to the king, East took his ace and returned a heart. I ruffed with my last trump. Now what about that club queen?

But wait! Here's where the light went on. West had opened a weak two hearts showing six of them. He had followed to three rounds of spades. What about diamonds? I played the queen and the jack, and West followed to all three. Eureka! He only had one club. I led a club to the king, West following with his SINGLETON deuce. I had read this in books. I led a club back and, with a flourish, played my nine...whereupon West took his club queen (!) and cashed the rest of his hearts for down three. Here was the entire hand:

**DLR: WEST      VUL: N-S**

```
                    ♠ A 10 6
                    ♡ A J
                    ◇ K Q 7 4
                    ♣ K 10 8 5

    ♠ 7 4 2              N              ♠ K 9 5
    ♡ K Q 10 9 7 2                      ♡ 8 6 5 3
    ◇ 8 3          W  ✦  E              ◇ A 10 6 5
    ♣ Q 2                               ♣ 6 3
                        S
                    ♠ Q J 8 3
                    ♡ 4
                    ◇ J 9 2
                    ♣ A J 9 7 4
```

"What did you do," I asked West, dazed and shaken, "open a weak two with only five hearts?"

"Never," he said.

"Then where's your third diamond?

"Didn't have one," he said. " I pitched a heart on the third one."

"I didn't see it," I told Claudia, crushed. "That's a shame. I had that hand all counted out too."

"Mm," she said. "I guess before you can count, you have to learn the difference between hearts and diamonds, huh?"

♠ ♡ ◊ ♣

C H A P T E R     5 5
# A Game of Inferences - Part I

*Crime is common. Logic is rare. Therefore it is upon the logic rather than upon the crime that you should dwell.*
- Sir Arthur Conan Doyle
The Adventures of Sherlock Holmes

Bridge is a game of inferences. If you enjoy solving puzzles or working out problems, then this is the game for you.

In his preface to *Better Bridge for the Advancing Player*, Frank Stewart tells us that nobody can play and enjoy this game by blindly following any set of rules. "The appeal of the game lies in the almost infinite variety of problem situations the players may face. This is definitely a thinking person's game, and learning how to think is important."

Later Stewart says that the emphasis of his book is on drawing inferences from the opponents' bidding and play. Everybody in today's game loves to bid, and often it is inferences drawn from all of this bidding that will guide declarer to the winning line of play. Observe this hand from Fred L. Karpin's book, *The Art of Card Reading at Bridge*.

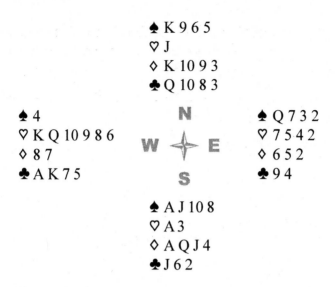

```
              ♠ K 9 6 5
              ♡ J
              ◊ K 10 9 3
              ♣ Q 10 8 3

  ♠ 4              N            ♠ Q 7 3 2
  ♡ K Q 10 9 8 6                ♡ 7 5 4 2
  ◊ 8 7        W  ✦  E          ◊ 6 5 2
  ♣ A K 7 5                     ♣ 9 4
                   S
              ♠ A J 10 8
              ♡ A 3
              ◊ A Q J 4
              ♣ J 6 2
```

South gets to a contract of FOUR SPADES after West bids hearts twice ostensibly announcing the possession of no fewer than six hearts. West then leads the ace and king of clubs, East ruffs the third round and returns a heart. How should South play the spades? Now that there are only three of them outstanding, should he cash the ace and king hoping to fell the queen? As you can see in this layout he would fail. But wait, there is some logic to be applied here- an inference to be drawn.

South could <u>see</u> that West had four clubs, and he could <u>hear</u> that he was almost certain to have six hearts. Thus West was dealt a maximum of three cards in diamonds and spades. Any missing key card figures to be in the hand containing the greater number of unknown cards, so South leads the jack of spades from his hand to entice West to cover in case he does possess the queen. When West follows with the four, South, heeding the inference he has drawn, overtakes with the spade king and leads the nine of spades back to his hand finessing East's queen.

Karpin says that, in theory, West could have been void in diamonds and held Qxx of spades, but "percentage is percentage is percentage" (I wonder if Karpin knew Gertrude Stein) and there was a 70% chance that East held the queen.

Some might consider West's second bid the crime that led South to the correct line of play. Bids and overcalls are not a crime, though. You can hardly survive in today's game without being an active bidder. But when those bids are made, it is incumbent upon the improving declarer to make good use of the information.

Observe. Playing against a solid pair at a sectional tournament, I encountered this wild deal:

**Dlr: North      Vul: None**

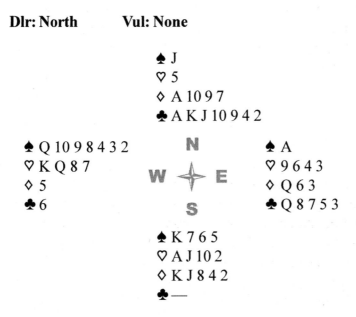

```
                    ♠ J
                    ♡ 5
                    ◊ A 10 9 7
                    ♣ A K J 10 9 4 2

 ♠ Q 10 9 8 4 3 2           N           ♠ A
 ♡ K Q 8 7                               ♡ 9 6 4 3
 ◊ 5              W   ✧   E               ◊ Q 6 3
 ♣ 6                                     ♣ Q 8 7 5 3
                           S
                    ♠ K 7 6 5
                    ♡ A J 10 2
                    ◊ K J 8 4 2
                    ♣ —
```

My partner, North, opened ONE CLUB. I responded ONE DIA-MOND, and West doubled. My partner, with two singletons, bid THREE DIAMONDS. I, for some reason, fell in love with my hand and bid SIX DIAMONDS.

West led a spade. East took his ace and returned a heart. Oh oh. I was going to have to find the queen of diamonds. Let's see...eight ever, nine never? You've heard the little rhyme, haven't you? As you can see, though, if I do that here, I go down. Wait, were there any inferences to be drawn? West doubled suggesting the possession of at least ten cards in the major suits. That left only three clubs and diamonds. The odds were that East held the diamond queen. Just in case, I led the diamond jack out of my hand. Even though I knew West would duck smoothly with Qx, I still heeded the inference I had drawn, took the ace, led the diamond ten from dummy and closed my eyes. When I opened them, there was a spade on the table in front of West. Whew!

The rest was easy. To keep my transportation open with dummy, I next played the clubs from the top, trapped East's queen with a ruffing finesse, drew the last trump, got to dummy with a ruff and the rest of the clubs were good.

True, you might think West's bid was a crime. Some number of spades might have been best, jamming our bidding and giving less of a clue about West's distribution. But there it was- information to be used to help with the play of the hand. And, if you're like me, you can use all the help you can get!

So next time you play, forget those nursery rhymes. Keep your eyes and ears open, do a little sleuthing, and see if you can begin to take your game to the next level.

♠ ♡ ◇ ♣

# C H A P T E R  5 6
# A Game of Inferences - Part II

*You see, but you do not observe.*
- Sir Arthur Conan Doyle
The Adventures of Sherlock Holmes

So, you'd like to improve your bridge game. You've taken some
lessons, you've found a compatible partner, you've added one
or two gadgets to your bidding, you play once, maybe twice a week at
local clubs, and you might have even gone to a tournament or two.

Sometimes you do well, and sometimes you don't. It all seems like a
crapshoot to you, something beyond your control. Some players never
get past this level of bridge, but you have the feeling there must be something more, some way to take your game to the next level.

Fred L. Karpin in *The Art of Card Reading at Bridge* says that in
his opinion, "if one were able to put his finger on the exact point where the
average player undergoes a qualitative change and starts up the road leading
to the development of a good bridge player, that point would be where
the average player is no longer immersed in his own cards, and simulta-
neously he begins to pay close attention to the bidding of the opponents
and the clues contained therein."

In other words, you have to do more than <u>see</u> at the bridge table; you
also must <u>observe</u>. You have to stop playing by rules and little nursery
rhymes, and you have to learn how to think. Here was a case in point that
I encountered recently at our club. I picked up: ♠: 7 ♡: Q ◇: Q 10 8 4 3
2 ♣: A K 8 4 3. At equal vulnerability, RHO opened the bidding with
ONE HEART. I overcalled 2NT, unusual, showing the minors. LHO bid

THREE HEARTS, and my partner came in with FOUR HEARTS telling me that I could pick my best minor. After inquiring about the bid, RHO bid FIVE HEARTS. Knowing that we had a double fit in the minors, I bid SIX DIAMONDS, which was passed out.

Hmm. I had bid this as a sacrifice more than anything else and certainly expected to be doubled. LHO led the Ace of Spades, and here is what I saw:

| | |
|---|---|
| ♠: 7 | ♠: Q108 |
| ♡: Q | ♡: A 9 |
| ◇: Q 10 8 4 3 2 | ◇: A J 9 5 |
| ♣: A K 8 4 3 | ♣: 10 9 7 5 |

RHO played the 5 of spades on the ace, LHO shifted to a heart, and I took the ace. So there I was. I had done it again. East-West certainly were not making five hearts. As I paused to consider my next move, my partner had that wounded look on his face, which said "This is going to be another bottom, isn't it?"

So, how would you play the hand and justify your bidding? I'll tell you this much. Par on this hand was 6 DIAMONDS doubled going down one or two. Of course.

All I had to do was pass FIVE HEARTS around to my partner who would have doubled, and we would have collected 300 or maybe even 500. But no. Here I was in 6 DIAMONDS. Great.

Hold on. This is a game of inferences, remember? And West had kindly presented me with all of the information I needed to make the hand. He had led the ace of spades. East had opened the bidding, I had 22 points in my combined hands, and the spade ace brought the total to 26. If West had the king of diamonds, then East would have opened the bidding with only eleven points and a very ratty heart suit.

She had to have the king of diamonds, and in order for me to make this hand, it had to be singleton. So, I called for the diamond ace. East gave me an annoyed look and dropped her stiff king on the table. That was one hurdle, but I wasn't out of the woods yet. What about clubs? Maybe I could learn something by ruffing a spade. I led the ten and RHO played the jack. Hmm. I drew the last trump ending in dummy and led the ten of clubs. RHO played the queen! Was she splitting her honors? Did she have the doubleton queen-jack? Wouldn't that be nice? I took my ace, went back to dummy with a trump, and led the club nine. East followed with the six. What would you do?

To be honest with you, I didn't have a clue. There was that look from partner again as I pondered RHO's low club lying on the table in front of me. I always got this wrong. But wait. There was another inference here, wasn't there? LHO had responded at the three level. He had to have six points. What could they be? RHO had the spade jack and surely the king. LHO must have the heart jack and the club jack for his bid. I flew with the king of clubs. NO WAIT! Couldn't LHO have the Ace of spades, the jack of hearts, and a singleton club? Wouldn't he have supported partner's hearts with five points and a singleton? Too late. I had played my king. Here was the full deal:

**DLR: East       VUL: NONE**

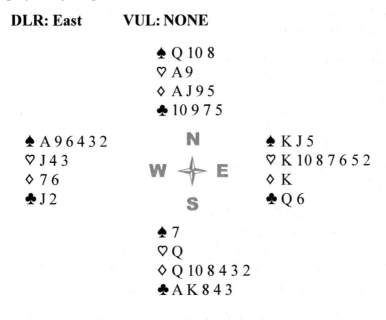

```
              ♠ Q 10 8
              ♡ A 9
              ◊ A J 9 5
              ♣ 10 9 7 5
♠ A 9 6 4 3 2               ♠ K J 5
♡ J 4 3                     ♡ K 10 8 7 6 5 2
◊ 7 6                       ◊ K
♣ J 2                       ♣ Q 6
              ♠ 7
              ♡ Q
              ◊ Q 10 8 4 3 2
              ♣ A K 8 4 3
```

LHO's jack of clubs hit the table, and all was well.

"Nicely played," said partner. His woebegone look was transformed into a blissful smile.

I didn't say a word. In some cases, North played the hand, got a sneaky queen of clubs lead from East and, without any further information to go on, took the doomed diamond finesse. Later they misguessed the clubs. There were some South's, though, who got the same lead I did and still took the diamond finesse. That made me feel pretty good.

But what about the clubs, you ask. Well, sometimes you just have to be lucky, don't you? Eight ever, nine never. Hey, do you think there's something to that little rhyme?

♠ ♡ ◇ ♣

C H A P T E R     5 7
# A Game of Inferences - Part III

*It has long been an axiom of mine that the little things*
*are infinitely the most important.*
- Sir Arthur Conan Doyle
The Adventures of Sherlock Holmes

Enough! You're sick and tired of below-average bridge games, of getting kicked around by more experienced players, of being regarded as nothing more than cannon fodder when you arrive at the opponents' table.

You've come to realize that bridge is indeed a game of inferences. You've tried to pay more attention to your opponents' bids and the clues that they might contain. You're no longer just bidding your own cards and following suit in your own little world. You've learned to draw inferences from your opponents' actions. You have actually started down the road to learning how to think at the bridge table.

So what happened to you on this recent deal from your club?

**VUL: N-SDLR: NORTH**

```
              ♠ Q J 9 5
              ♡ A Q 6
              ◊ A 8
              ♣ J 9 5 4

♠ —                          ♠ K 10 6 2
♡ 9 5 4 3         N          ♡ K 2
◊ 9 7 6 4 3 2   W ✦ E        ◊ K Q J 5
♣ Q 8 6           S          ♣ K 10 3

              ♠ A 8 7 4 3
              ♡ J 10 8 7
              ◊ 10
              ♣ A 7 2
```

It's just a little part-score, not a slam or even a game. But the majority of duplicate bridge sessions are comprised of deals just such as this, and you, the improving player, need to realize that they are just as important as games or even slams. Here was the bidding on this deal:

| North | East | South | West |
|-------|------|-------|------|
|       |      | (You) |      |
| 1 ♣   | DBL  | 1 ♠   | PASS |
| 2 ♠   | ALL PASS |   |      |

West led the six of clubs. You tried the nine and East played the ten. You weren't sure what was going on in clubs. East doubled clubs and should therefore be short. You were worried about a ruff, so you took your ace right away, crossed to the ace of diamonds and got the spades going by leading the queen. East covered, you won your ace and saw the expected bad split.

Still worried about a club ruff, you continued with a spade back to your jack and a third spade. East won with his ten and tried to cash the king of diamonds which you ruffed. You now decided to take the heart finesse (careful!) and led the jack from your hand (no!). East won, returned his last spade, and there you were:

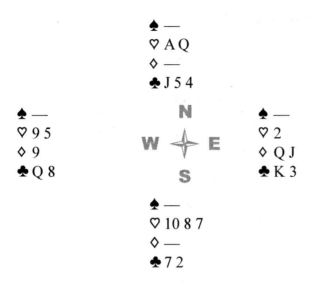

Now you saw it, didn't you? You had won four spade tricks, the ace of diamonds and the ace of clubs. You could take your ace and queen of hearts to make two, but the opponents would have the rest when this hand was cold for three. You could have assured nine tricks by leading a low heart from your hand and playing the queen. Then the suit wouldn't have been blocked, and you could have gotten back to your hand and your long heart. But no. You severed your own communication.

And you knew, didn't you, that East was likely to have the heart king anyway because of his double? That was the inference you should have drawn, wasn't it? No matter. All was well. Your partner opened the traveler, and two spades making two was tied for a top. It seems that East-West could make three or four diamonds, and all East had to do was overcall either ONE DIAMOND or ONE NO TRUMP for them to get to their top spot.

But that didn't make you feel any better, did it? There was no satisfaction in getting a good score when you didn't play good bridge.

After the game, you overheard the other spade declarer bemoaning the fact that he had blocked the hearts just as you had when he knew, just knew, that East had the king. You knew it too, didn't you?

All right, all right. I admit it. This didn't happen to you, it happened to me. But you wouldn't want to do the same, would you? It's paying attention to the little things, the little hands as well as the big ones, and the little details contained therein that will eventually improve your play.

♠ ♡ ◇ ♣

C H A P T E R     5 8
# The Field

*It's what a fellow thinks he knows that hurts him.*
- Kin Hubbard

So you want to play duplicate bridge? You know the game of bridge- how to bid, how to declare, how to defend. You learned the game in college, perhaps. You picked it up again years later when friends of yours said they played, or maybe there was a group at work who played during the lunch hour.

Then you saw the article in your local paper. There was a duplicate bridge club that met every Tuesday. Why not? You knew the game. You could do this. So, with high expectations you and your wife took some lessons that were offered at the local high school, and off you went one Tuesday night. And another. And another. And you kept getting hammered- chalking up a series of below-average games. What was wrong? You knew the game, didn't you?

Duplicate, however, is an altogether different animal. In duplicate, there was one thing you had to consider, which made no difference at all in other forms of scoring- THE FIELD. What was everyone else in your direction going to do with your cards? How would they bid them? How would they play them? According to Kay, Silodor and Karpin in *The Complete Book of Duplicate Bridge*, "In rubber bridge, one lives in his own little world, and there is just one enemy, at his left flank and at his right. In duplicate bridge, one cannot afford to be an 'isolationist'; that is, he cannot live his life 'far from the madding crowd's ignoble strife.'" Your main consideration is always the quest for supremacy over your competitors, and you must constantly keep in mind what they- THE FIELD- did with your hand. Are you in a good contract or a bad one, a normal or an abnormal one?

Here's an example from Kay, Silodor, and Karpin:

**DLR: NORTH   VUL: NONE**

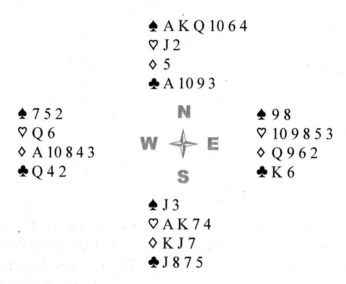

&spades; A K Q 10 6 4
&hearts; J 2
&diams; 5
&clubs; A 10 9 3

&spades; 7 5 2
&hearts; Q 6
&diams; A 10 8 4 3
&clubs; Q 4 2

&spades; 9 8
&hearts; 10 9 8 5 3
&diams; Q 9 6 2
&clubs; K 6

&spades; J 3
&hearts; A K 7 4
&diams; K J 7
&clubs; J 8 7 5

As South, you wind up in 3NT and win the diamond lead with your king. You can see that most pairs would be playing FOUR SPADES rather than 3NT. At the 4 spade contract, 11 tricks will be made unless East has *both* the king and queen of clubs. So what good are ten tricks at no trump (plus 430) if most pairs make 11 tricks at spades (plus 450)? You must play for eleven tricks even if it jeopardizes your contract.

The best play is to lead a low heart at trick two toward dummy's jack. If West has the queen, the board's jack will become your eleventh trick. If East has the queen, however, back will come a diamond and down you go. No matter, bidding 3NT and making four would have given you very few matchpoints anyway.

A session of duplicate bridge is rife with such decisions and considerations. Pay them no heed, and you're headed for the bottom of the pack. Yeah, sure. So where was I when this deal came up recently at the club?

**DLR: NORTH   VUL: NORTH-SOUTH**

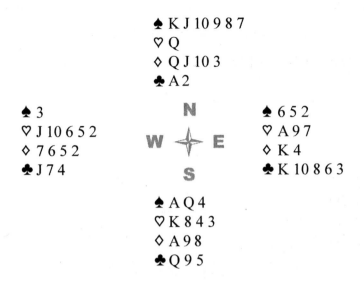

                    ♠ K J 10 9 8 7
                    ♡ Q
                    ◊ Q J 10 3
                    ♣ A 2

    ♠ 3                              ♠ 6 5 2
    ♡ J 10 6 5 2                     ♡ A 9 7
    ◊ 7 6 5 2                        ◊ K 4
    ♣ J 7 4                          ♣ K 10 8 6 3

                    ♠ A Q 4
                    ♡ K 8 4 3
                    ◊ A 9 8
                    ♣ Q 9 5

My partner opened ONE SPADE with the North hand. Ha! I had
seen this before. I had read about the beauty of bidding 3NT with a
hand like South's. So 3NT it was. Sitting West was Bob Rosenberg,
a fine player and a frequent partner. He shrugged and led his fourth
best heart. Why couldn't he have led a diamond? East took his ace
and returned a heart. So there I was. What would you do? My only
thought was why partner hadn't taken me back to 4 SPADES with his six
card suit.

I held up for one more round of hearts, then played spades and took
the diamond finesse. All was well, and I made 5…for a zero. Everyone,
of course, was making six spades losing only to the ace of hearts. As my
partner wrote in our bottom score on the traveler, I couldn't help asking
him why he hadn't rebid his six card suit. We belong in spades, I told him,
passing the proverbial buck.

"That's irrelevant, isn't it?" said Rosenberg, not letting me get away
with blaming partner. "At trick one you should have realized that THE
FIELD would be in four spades making six if the diamond finesse is on.
You take your king of hearts at trick two, you run the spades, and you
take the diamond finesse. If it loses, you haven't lost much anyway. Nice
little lesson hand, isn't it?"

"Thanks, Bob."

♠ ♡ ◇ ♣

P A R T  F I V E
# Defense

Defense is easily the most challenging aspect of the game of bridge. In other sports, you can see what the offense is up to, you can see your fellow defenders, and you can adjust your play accordingly.

In basketball, never give your opponent an open lane to the basket. Keep your hands up. Watch your opponent's hips. Slide your feet. Don't cross your legs. Double team their top scorer. Help out underneath on the weak side. Block out your opponents for rebounds. Keep your eye on your man.

In football, control the line of scrimmage and pressure the offense. Force them to make mistakes. Watch film, study the opponents' formations and tendencies. Watch the quarterback's eyes. Jam their receivers at the line. Stay at home. Keep your eye on your man.

In hockey, take the body. Don't get in the habit of watching the puck. Never outnumber your opponents behind the net. They can not score from there. Pick up the open player in front of the net. Stay at home. Keep your eye on your man.

But here you are at the bridge table. You can see only the dummy, and not even that if you must make the opening lead.

In his book *Defensive Bridge Play Complete*, Eddie Kantar says "the average player doesn't even realize how many tricks slip by through faulty signaling and discarding, 'unlucky' leads, and failing to count."

H.W. Kelsey in *Killing Defence at Bridge* says, "the average defender operates under a fog of uncertainty. He makes elementary mistakes...due to faulty logic, failure to count, and failure to draw simple inferences. The very fact that there are two defenders makes a defensive error twice as likely."

So here you are, on the defense. Are you ready to apply some logic, do some counting, and draw some inferences? Have you been listening to the bidding? Are you ready to make that opening lead? Do you have those excuses all lined up?

GIVE ME A "D"...

CHAPTER 5 9
# Upperclassmen

*What I often forget about students, especially undergraduates,*
*is that surface appearances are misleading. Most of them*
*are at base as conventional as Presbyterian deacons.*
- Muriel Bradle

According to Charles Goren in *Goren's New Bridge Complete*, many colorful expressions from all walks of life ultimately find their way into the picturesque language of bridge. One of those is the "uppercut" borrowed from boxing and used to describe the trumping of one of your partner's cards, even though it may be a winner, in order to force out a higher trump from declarer. This is done with the hope of building up a trump trick for partner. For instance:

```
                   ♠ 8 7 5 3
                   ◇ Q 6 3 2
                         N
    ♠ J 6                          ♠ Q 9
    ◇ A K J 10 4    W  ✦  E        ◇ 9 8
                         S
                   ♠ A K 10 4 2
                   ◇ 7 5
```

If spades are trumps, West plays the ace, king and jack of diamonds. East ruffs the jack with his spade queen even if the diamond is not covered and promotes West's jack of spades to a trick.

When I taught an introduction to duplicate bridge class recently, I explained <u>none</u> of this to my beginners. So when two of my students came to my table at the club recently, I was not prepared to be uppercut by them.  Here was the hand:

**DLR: SOUTH    VUL: N-S**

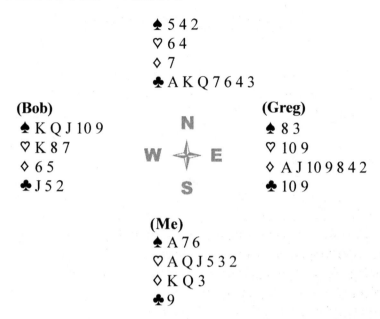

♠ 5 4 2
♡ 6 4
♢ 7
♣ A K Q 7 6 4 3

**(Bob)**
♠ K Q J 10 9
♡ K 8 7
♢ 6 5
♣ J 5 2

**(Greg)**
♠ 8 3
♡ 10 9
♢ A J 10 9 8 4 2
♣ 10 9

**(Me)**
♠ A 7 6
♡ A Q J 5 3 2
♢ K Q 3
♣ 9

I was South, and my two students, Greg and Bob were East-West. After a spirited round of bidding in which all four of us bid our suits, I wound up in a contract of FOUR HEARTS, and Bob led the king of spades. Oh oh. I could lose two spades, a diamond and one or more hearts. I took the spade ace, led a club to dummy and pitched a spade on the king of clubs. Should I lead the queen of clubs and pitch my last spade?

Then I would lose the ruff, and possibly two diamonds and two hearts. So I led a diamond. Greg took his ace and led a spade. Bob won his 9 and returned the queen of spades. I ruffed. As you can see, I could now get home by laying down the Ace and queen of hearts. But no, not me, not if there was a finesse to be taken. I ruffed my good diamond queen and led a heart. Bob won with the king and led the jack of spades. Here was the position:

(useless clubs)

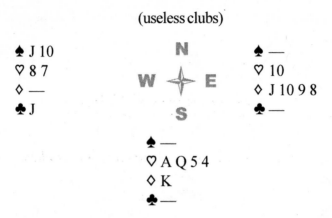

```
        ♠ J 10              N              ♠ —
        ♡ 8 7                              ♡ 10
        ◇ —            W  ✦  E            ◇ J 10 9 8
        ♣ J                 S              ♣ —

                          ♠ —
                          ♡ A Q 5 4
                          ◇ K
                          ♣ —
```

All right! I was going to make this and not look bad in front of my students. But wait. Greg ruffed with his ten of hearts promoting Bob's 8 to the setting trick!

"Why did you ruff?" I asked Greg. "Didn't you know his spade jack was good?"

"Sure," he said, "but my heart wasn't any good. I thought I might as well use it. Was that wrong?"

"Oh no," I said as my partner tallied up the only positive East-West score on this board. "Not at all."

C H A P T E R    6 0
# Uppercut City

*The most important thing in communication is to hear
what isn't being said.*
- Peter Drucker

Whether I teach communication in my English classes, I explain
that it requires four elements: a sender, a receiver, a message,
and a medium. Remove any of these components, and communication is
not possible. I would have done well to remember that lesson myself
when I encountered this problem at the club.

My partner and I came to Bruce's table. Bruce was a longtime player
and a crafty opponent. One of our club's top players, Daryl, did not have
a partner that night and was kibitzing at Bruce's table. Here was our first
board:

**DLR: EAST    VUL: N-S**

```
                    ♠ 10 5
                    ♡ Q 5 4
                    ◊ J 10 5 3
                    ♣ A 10 4 2
    ♠ 7 2              N              ♠ Q J 9 8 4 3
    ♡ A 10 2                          ♡ -
    ◊ K 4 2        W  ✦  E            ◊ A Q 9 8 7
    ♣ K 9 8 5 3        S              ♣ J 7
                    ♠ A K 6
                    ♡ K J 9 8 7 6 3
                    ◊ 6
                    ♣ Q 6
```

I was South and Bruce was West on this hand. East opened TWO SPADES. I bid THREE HEARTS. THREE SPADES from Bruce. FOUR HEARTS from my partner, which was passed out.

Bruce didn't "take the sac," as he called sacrificing, at FOUR SPADES, so he must have thought he could set me. I got a spade lead and waited anxiously for the dummy to hit. Hmm. I counted my tricks—ten with a spade ruff. What could go wrong? Nothing here to impress Daryl the kibitzer with. It looked like ol' Bruce should have taken the sacrifice after all. As you will see, however, I was right the first time. Ol' Bruce was pretty sure I was goin' down.

I played the ace and king of spades and ruffed a spade. Bruce pitched a club. I then led the queen of hearts. Bruce's partner pitched a high diamond, and Bruce played the two of hearts. No problem, I thought. I would still lose a heart, a club, and a diamond.

I played a second heart to my king and Bruce's ace. He then led a diamond to his partner's ace, and back came a spade from East. Oh, oh. Now I saw it. Here was the end position in hearts:

**(Bruce)**
♡ 10

**(Carl)**
♡ J 9 8 7 6

No matter what I played, Bruce would score his ten of hearts.

"Welcome to uppercut city," said ol' Bruce, the ol' fox.

I ruffed with the 9 and Bruce overruffed. He exited with the king of diamonds, and I had to lose a club later for down one. We opened the traveling score. One pair had lost only 300 points with a spade sacrifice, but everyone else had made FOUR HEARTS. I was sure that none of them had someone like ol' Bruce setting up an uppercut against them, though.

"Is there any way I can make the hand?" I asked Daryl.

"Sure," he replied. "When you play the queen of hearts and find out the trump situation, you should see the uppercut coming. Lead a diamond right then. That cuts the opponents' communication. If East wins and leads a spade, you still have a trump in dummy, so you throw your losing club on the spade. Bruce makes his ten of hearts, but your club loser is gone."

The key, I realized, was *communication*. Bruce was the *sender*, his partner was the *receiver*, and the *message* was "Lead another spade, and let's uppercut ol' Carl." All I had to do was remove the *medium*- the diamond- their means of communication. If I had done that I could have really impressed Daryl, and I would not have received such a warm welcome to uppercut city.

# CHAPTER 61
# Entries - Part I

*The trouble with him was that he was without imagination.*
*He was quick and alert in the things of life, but only*
*the things, and not in the significances.*
- Jack London "To Build a Fire"

In a typical bridge session, you will declare some of the hands and so will your partner, but for about half of the evening the two of you will be on defense, struggling in the dark, trying not to let another unmakeable contract slip through. It therefore stands to reason that your overall game will improve if you can tighten up what experts call the most difficult part of bridge- defense.

One of my partners, Bob Rosenberg, says that a glaring weakness in my defense is recognizing and attacking entries to long, dangerous side suits. There are even times when you must deliberately sacrifice a high card to dislodge an entry to the danger suit. This play is known as a Merrimack Coup, named after a coal ship, The Merrimack, which was scuttled by the U.S. Navy during the Spanish-American War in one of the Cuban harbor channels to neutralize the Spanish ships in port. In the same manner, the sacrifice of a high card neutralizes the danger suit.

Observe this example from Frank Stewart's *Winning Defense For The Advancing Bridge Player.* You are East and hear this bidding:

| North | East | South | West |
|-------|------|-------|------|
| —     | —    | 1 ♡   | PASS |
| 2 ◊   | P ASS | 2 ♡  | PASS |
| 2 NT  | P ASS | 3 NT | ALL PASS |

Partner leads the 6 of spades (fourth best) and you see:

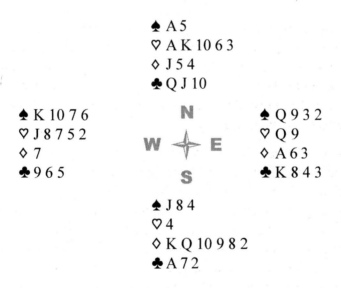

♠ A 5
♡ A K 10 6 3
◊ J 5 4
♣ Q J 10

            N                    ♠ Q 9 3 2
                                 ♡ Q 9
    W   ✦   E                    ◊ A 6 3
            S                    ♣ K 8 4 3

After some thought, declarer plays low and you win the queen. What next? The whole deal:

♠ A 5
♡ A K 10 6 3
◊ J 5 4
♣ Q J 10

♠ K 10 7 6              N                    ♠ Q 9 3 2
♡ J 8 7 5 2                                  ♡ Q 9
◊ 7           W   ✦   E                      ◊ A 6 3
♣ 9 6 5                S                     ♣ K 8 4 3

            ♠ J 8 4
            ♡ 4
            ◊ K Q 10 9 8 2
            ♣ A 7 2

Based on the bidding, could you visualize the danger suit in declarer's hand? Could you also visualize the only entry to it, the ace of clubs? If you switch to your king of clubs, declarer must go down. If he takes his ace, you hold off the diamond ace for two rounds and kill the suit. If he ducks, you switch back to spades and set declarer with 3 spades, a diamond and a club.

I, however, even have trouble with entries and danger suits when they are clearly visible in dummy and no flamboyant high card sacrifice is required. Here was a recent hand from the club. I was East defending

3NT against two of my former students, so the pressure was on. My partner, Bob, led the ten of clubs, and I saw:

&spades; A K 8 7 2
&hearts; A 6 2
&diams; 6 5 3
&clubs; J 4

&spades; 6 4 3
&hearts; J 10 9 8 3
&diams; 8 2
&clubs; A K 6

What would you do? I played the ace, king and another club. Hand over. Here was the entire deal:

**DLR: SOUTH    VUL: N-S**

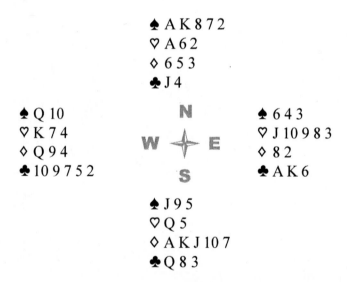

&spades; A K 8 7 2
&hearts; A 6 2
&diams; 6 5 3
&clubs; J 4

&spades; Q 10
&hearts; K 7 4
&diams; Q 9 4
&clubs; 10 9 7 5 2

&spades; 6 4 3
&hearts; J 10 9 8 3
&diams; 8 2
&clubs; A K 6

&spades; J 9 5
&hearts; Q 5
&diams; A K J 10 7
&clubs; Q 8 3

Declarer won the club queen, and led the jack of spades. Bob covered, and declarer played the king, the ace, and won the third round in hand with the 9. Back to the ace of hearts to enjoy the spades and, eschewing the diamond finesse, made three. If I had seen the danger suit (spades) and the entry (the ace of hearts), I could have switched to the jack of hearts at trick two and neutralized the spade suit. Declarer could have unblocked the 9 of spades under the king (would he have done that?), but he would have still had only had eight tricks.

The field, of course, was in FOUR SPADES which fails when East on lead makes the same heart switch at trick two. THREE NO TRUMP down two would have been a top for us rather than the bottom we got for allowing it to make.

"Carl…" my partner began after South wrapped up nine tricks.

"I know, I know," I said. "The entry."

# C H A P T E R   6 2
# Entries - Part II

*When you lose, don't lose the lesson.*
*The Dalai Lama*

I n the last chapter, I told you about the weakest part of my defensive game-my inability to recognize and attack entries to long, dangerous side suits. There are even times when you need to sacrifice a high card of your own to cut declarer's transportation to that side suit. Here's another example from Frank Stewart's *Winning Defense For The Advancing Bridge Player* where you have to recognize the side suit and attack the entry to it:

<pre>
        ♠ K Q 4 3
        ♡ 8 6 3
        ◇ K Q 10 7 6
        ♣ Q

            N              ♠ A J 10 8
                           ♡ 10 5 2
        W  ✦  E            ◇ A 5 4 2
                           ♣ A 10
            S
</pre>

Partner leads the 9 of clubs against 3NT. How do you defend? Here's the entire deal:

```
                        ♠ K Q 4 3
                        ♡ 8 6 3
                        ◊ K Q 10 7 6
                        ♣ Q
        ♠ 7 6 5          N           ♠ A J 10 8
        ♡ Q 9 7                      ♡ 10 5 2
        ◊ 8         W  ✦  E          ◊ A 5 4 2
        ♣ 9 8 7 6 5 2    S           ♣ A 10
                        ♠ 9 2
                        ♡ A K J 4
                        ◊ J 9 3
                        ♣ K J 4 3
```

At trick two you must return the jack of spades. This gives declarer his spade winner before he's ready to use it to get to the diamonds, and the most he can make is 8 tricks.

I know all this. I've read the books. I've listened to one of my partners, Bob Rosenberg, who keeps exhorting me to "attack the entry." So why do these things keep happening? As South, I held: ♠: A K J 6 3 ♡: 7 4 2 ◊: J 10 2 ♣: 7 6. West was the dealer and this was the bidding:

| West | North | East | South |
|------|-------|------|-------|
| 1 ♣  | 1 ♠   | 2 ♡  | 4 ♠   |
| 5 ♡  | PASS  | PASS | PASS  |

I led the ace of spades and saw:

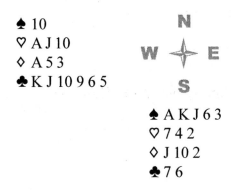

```
        ♠ 10              N
        ♡ A J 10
        ◊ A 5 3      W  ✦  E
        ♣ K J 10 9 6 5    S
                        ♠ A K J 6 3
                        ♡ 7 4 2
                        ◊ J 10 2
                        ♣ 7 6
```

Partner played the 9 of spades on my ace. What would you do next? A club, playing partner for the ace-queen? What about a heart? Yes, a heart! Declarer will want to ruff a spade, and a heart switch now might get his transportation tangled up.

Wait, Carl! The side suit! The entry! Too late- I led the heart. The whole deal:

**DLR: WEST     VUL: NONE**

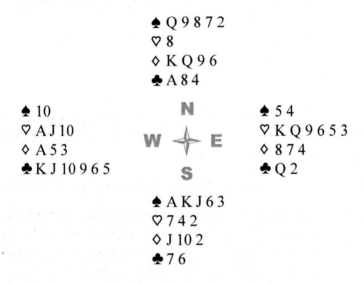

```
                    ♠ Q 9 8 7 2
                    ♡ 8
                    ◇ K Q 9 6
                    ♣ A 8 4
    ♠ 10                              ♠ 5 4
    ♡ A J 10            N             ♡ K Q 9 6 5 3
    ◇ A 5 3        W   ✦   E          ◇ 8 7 4
    ♣ K J 10 9 6 5      S             ♣ Q 2
                    ♠ A K J 6 3
                    ♡ 7 4 2
                    ◇ J 10 2
                    ♣ 7 6
```

Declarer overtook the ten of hearts, ruffed a spade in dummy with the ace, overtook the jack, drew the last trump and led his queen of clubs. The diamond ace was his ENTRY to the clubs- making five. Look what happens if I switch to diamonds at trick two. Declarer must lose two diamonds, a club and a spade.

"Carl…" my partner began when the hand was over.

"I know, I know. The entry."

"Maybe it was my fault," Bob said. "If I had dropped the spade queen on the first trick, then maybe you would have woken up and re-membered the lesson."

♠ ♡ ◇ ♣

# C H A P T E R   6 3
# **Rules**

*The Golden Rule is that there are no golden rules.*
- George Bernard Shaw

When we learn the great game of bridge, we are taught a list of rules. You need 13 points to open, 6 to respond. Cover an honor with an honor. Eight ever, nine never.

Get the kiddies off the street. Second hand low. Third hand high.

As we all know, there are exceptions to every one of these rules. So why have rules if you are going to have exceptions? My English students ask me the same thing. "Write *ie* when the sound is e except after *c*" right? Except in seize, either, weird, leisure, and neither. But why have exceptions? Because, I tell my students, these are not rules, they are simply guidelines or explanations for the way things are most of the time. The same is true in bridge. Let's look at the last two guidelines mentioned above.

You are defending a contract of 3 SPADES. Sitting West, you lead a spade (I tried the sneaky 10), and you see:

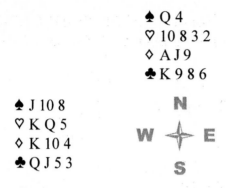

Declarer wins your spade and, paying no attention to your sneaky lead, draws trumps in two more rounds. He then leads a club to his king. Partner takes his ace and returns a club which declarer ruffs. He then leads a diamond toward the AJ9. Quick. Your play.

I went up with the king. Here was the entire hand:

**DLR: NORTH    VUL: N-S**

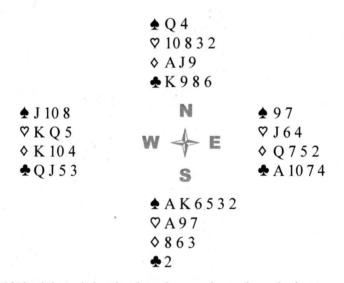

If I had thoughtlessly played second man low, declarer could insert the 9 and take two diamond tricks with a second round finesse. As it was, declarer won dummy's diamond ace. When he later led toward dummy's J9 of diamonds, I played low and he misguessed. The jack lost to partner's queen, and I still had to win the diamond 10. Down one gave us a tie for top.

Here is another hand, this one from one of the World Wide Bridge Contests. Partner leads the 5 of Hearts against a 3NT contract. You see:

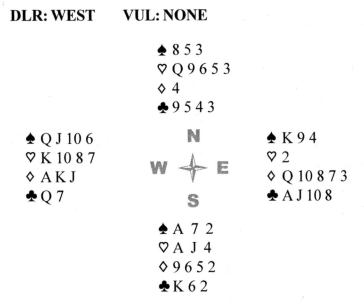

```
        N           ♠ K 9 4
     W  ✦  E        ♡ 2
        S           ◊ Q 10 8 7 3
                    ♣ A J 10 8
```

```
        ♠ A 7 2
        ♡ A J 4
        ◊ 9 6 5 2
        ♣ K 6 2
```

Declarer quickly calls for the heart in dummy. Your play! Quick! Here was the entire hand:

**DLR: WEST      VUL: NONE**

```
                    ♠ 8 5 3
                    ♡ Q 9 6 5 3
                    ◊ 4
                    ♣ 9 5 4 3

    ♠ Q J 10 6          N          ♠ K 9 4
    ♡ K 10 8 7                     ♡ 2
    ◊ A K J       W  ✦  E          ◊ Q 10 8 7 3
    ♣ Q 7              S           ♣ A J 10 8

                    ♠ A 7 2
                    ♡ A J 4
                    ◊ 9 6 5 2
                    ♣ K 6 2
```

I, sitting South, inserted the jack of hearts. What would you do as declarer? As you can see, the way to make this hand is duck three rounds of hearts. Easy to do if South plays the ace (third man high) and then the jack. Our declarer was down one giving us a 10 1/2 on a 12 top in our local game and 4437 matchpoints out of about 4800 in the world contest.

My biggest thrill was reading the analysis in the booklet of hands after the game. "3NT by West on a heart lead to the ace then duck the jack of hearts is 10 tricks–but if South plays the jack at trick one…"

So remember, don't just blindly follow those guidelines you were taught when you first took up the game of bridge. Instead, learn to THINK.

♠ ♡ ◇ ♣

C  H  A  P  T  E  R     6  4
# Sometimes a Great Notion

*A hunch is creativity trying to tell you something.*
*- Frank Capra*

*S*ometimes a Great Notion is the title of a Ken Kesey novel about the Oregon lumber industry. I wonder, though, if Kesey didn't have a bridge book in mind when he came up with that title- a book about opening leads.

Ah, the opening lead. The mystery of great mysteries in the world of bridge. How do you find that killing lead? And why is it your opponents always seem to find it against you, while you, on the other hand, manage to lead the only card that allows an otherwise doomed contract to make?

Many bridge writers have explored this bewildering topic. "Choosing the right suit to lead is one of the toughest problems in the game of bridge and often stumps even the experts," says Dorothy Truscott in *Bid Better, Play Better.* "The conservative player usually does best...at matchpoint play where the object is not necessarily to beat the contract but to prevent an overtrick," say Kay, Silodor and Karpin in *The Complete Book of Duplicate Bridge.* "All anyone can realistically hope for is opening leads that are consistently above average," says Frank Stewart in *Winning Defense for the Advancing Bridge Player.* Stewart then quotes golfer Bobby Jones (also a pretty good bridge player) who said, "Approximate squareness in striking the ball is all anyone can hope to attain." Stewart concludes that the luck factor makes the opening lead a pretty confounding part of the game.

Eddie Kantar best summarizes the difficulty of the opening lead in a chapter title of one of his books- *Lead as in Bleed.*

Actually, I think Kesey came closest to defining a good lead with his title. Every once in a while, you sometimes have a great notion. Consider this hand which I picked up in a knockout match:

♠: A J 10 8  ♡: 6 2  ◊: A 10 6 5  ♣: 6 3 2

I was South and listened to the following bidding:

| West | North | East | South |
|------|-------|------|-------|
| 1 ◊ | PASS | 1 ♡ | PASS |
| 2 ◊ | PASS | 4 ♡ | ALL PASS |

What would you have led? I thought that with my four diamonds, I might, based on the bidding, be able to give partner a ruff. I led the ace of diamonds. Here was the entire deal:

**DLR: WEST     VUL: NONE**

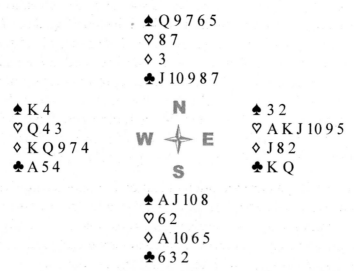

```
                    ♠ Q 9 7 6 5
                    ♡ 8 7
                    ◊ 3
                    ♣ J 10 9 8 7

     ♠ K 4                           ♠ 3 2
     ♡ Q 4 3            N            ♡ A K J 10 9 5
     ◊ K Q 9 7 4   W  ✛  E          ◊ J 8 2
     ♣ A 5 4            S            ♣ K Q

                    ♠ A J 10 8
                    ♡ 6 2
                    ◊ A 10 6 5
                    ♣ 6 3 2
```

Partner, perforce, played his diamond three. When I saw dummy, I thought I had made an egregious error. West, of course, should not have re-bid her five card diamond suit, but anyway it was too late to turn back now. I continued with the ten of diamonds, just in case, telling partner to return the highest of the remaining suits, spades, if he did indeed ruff, and so he did. I gave partner another ruff, and declarer was down one.

"Oh, come on guys," moaned the declarer.

"Why did you continue diamonds when all I had was the three?" partner asked.

"Once I led the ace," I said, "there really wasn't anything better to do."

"Gee," the declarer winced, "thanks for sharing that with me."

At the other table, FOUR HEARTS made five, and we won the match.

My favorite "notion" occurred one night at my club many moons ago against two flight A players. I was South and held: ♠: J 10 ♡: Q 8 4 ◊: 6 4 3 ♣: 9 6 5 3 2. My partner, North, opened ONE DIAMOND. RHO overcalled ONE SPADE. I passed, and LHO bid TWO SPADES, which ended the bidding. So, what would you have led? I chose a trump but saw no reason to lead the jack, so I led the ten of spades. When dummy came down with a doubleton club and the 965 of spades, I thought I might have hit on something. Sure enough, declarer used his only entry to dummy to finesse against what he thought was my partner's protected jack of spades. He needed to take a diamond finesse, but he no longer could, so he was the only declarer in the room to go down. After a lengthy post mortem with his partner, the two of them turned in my direction. "By the way," one of them acknowledged, "nice lead!"

Perhaps the greatest violation of Kay and Silodor's conservative approach to leads occurred on another night at my club. I was in FOUR HEARTS, and the player on lead, Harry, was notorious for his wild opening salvos- some spectacularly successful, and some dreadfully disastrous. Harry led a small diamond. Phew! I had three to the king. The lead couldn't hurt me. Down came the dummy with three trumps and a stiff jack of diamonds. I called for the jack and debated what I would do when the obvious trump shift occurred. RHO, however, followed with a low diamond! Harry had led low from the ace-queen of diamonds!

When the jack of diamonds held, I started to laugh, and Harry gave me a pleading look as if to say "please don't tell my partner what I just did."

"How in the world did you make five in that heart game?" my brother-in-law asked me after the game was over. You have three unavoidable losers.

"Endplay," I told him.

I wonder if old Harry ever read any Ken Kesey.

♠ ♡ ◇ ♣

# CHAPTER 65
# Fear

*The only thing we have to fear is fear itself.*
- Franklin Delano Roosevelt

Much has been written about the opening lead in bridge. The defense gets to fire the first salvo, which has the potential of either making or breaking a contract. Sometimes there are clues that point to a particular lead, but oftentimes it is simply a shot in the dark. It's always gratifying to hear "nice lead, partner," after a hand is over, but with me it is more often "Where did you come up with that lead?"

Theories abound about this mysterious aspect of the game:

- When in doubt, lead trump.
- Lead your partner's suit, and you won't lose the post mortem.
- Lead fourth from your longest and strongest.
- Lead third or fifth best.
- Don't lead from aces.
- Don't lead aces.
- Never lead from kings.
- Lead top of nothing.

I once asked one of NH's top masterpoint holders about his theory of opening leads. "At matchpoints, I tend to be conservative," he said. "That view has served me well over the years. In teams where overtricks don't much matter, I lead more aggressively. In duplicate, giving up an overtrick can be a disaster."

I adopted this philosophy, but unfortunately I took it one step further. My philosophy of opening leads is the philosophy of fear. Fear of giving up an overtrick or even the contract itself dominates my opening lead thinking. In one of his books, Eddie Kantar entitled the chapter about opening leads "Lead as in Bleed." My feelings exactly. Observe this recent hand from a club game.

**DLR: East**     **VUL: None**

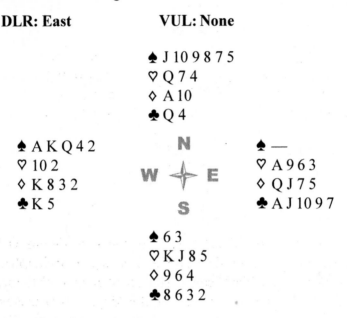

```
                    ♠ J 10 9 8 7 5
                    ♡ Q 7 4
                    ◇ A 10
                    ♣ Q 4
  ♠ A K Q 4 2              ♠ —
  ♡ 10 2                   ♡ A 9 6 3
  ◇ K 8 3 2                ◇ Q J 7 5
  ♣ K 5                    ♣ A J 10 9 7
                    ♠ 6 3
                    ♡ K J 8 5
                    ◇ 9 6 4
                    ♣ 8 6 3 2
```

I was South. East opened ONE CLUB, and then bid TWO DIAMONDS over West's response of ONE SPADE. West thought her partner had reversed showing a big hand, and she bid all the way to SIX DIAMONDS. My lead. Do you see that only a heart lead beats it, from the king-jack! If I lead a heart East can't get rid of her fourth heart on the spades (I ruff the third one) before she knocks out the ace of diamonds.

"Sorry partner," East said tallying up her 920, "I didn't mean to reverse.

"Oh, that's okay," said West sweetly. "Nicely played."

My opponents don't seem to suffer from my phobia. In another hand that same night:

**DLR: SOUTH   VUL: NONE**

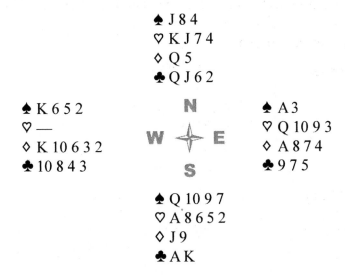

```
                    ♠ J 8 4
                    ♡ K J 7 4
                    ◊ Q 5
                    ♣ Q J 6 2
   ♠ K 6 5 2                        ♠ A 3
   ♡ —                              ♡ Q 10 9 3
   ◊ K 10 6 3 2                     ◊ A 8 7 4
   ♣ 10 8 4 3                       ♣ 9 7 5
                    ♠ Q 10 9 7
                    ♡ A 8 6 5 2
                    ◊ J 9
                    ♣ A K
```

Partner and I got to FOUR HEARTS on the North-South cards, a contract that was always going down. If West leads a passive club, though, (the lead at most other tables) I can win the ace of clubs, cash the ace of hearts getting the bad news, then cash the club king. Now I can cross to dummy's king of hearts and throw a diamond on the club queen. On the club jack, East can ruff if he wishes, but I throw my last diamond.

That was not what happened at our table. West led the 2 of spades! The play went spade ace, spade king, the return of the spade 6 for a spade ruff, low diamond (!) spade ruffed with the jack in dummy and overruffed with the queen, diamond ace. Down three for a zero.

"Why did you lead from the king of spades?" I asked West.

"Why not?" she said dauntlessly.

Aaargh!

# CHAPTER 66
# Aces and Patience

*Genius is nothing but a greater aptitude for patience*
- George Louis LeClerc de Buffon

"Aces are the most important cards in a bridge hand," I lectured my wife Claudia. "You have to be patient with aces. The fate of a hand often depends on how the declarer or the defender handles his aces."

"His?"

"Or hers. You know what I mean. When you open your hand and see an ace, a little bell should go off. It's time to be patient. Take this deal from a club game last month. I was playing with Rick. Look how he defended."

I drew the deal out for her on our kitchen pad:

```
              ♠ Q J 9
              ♡ 10 7 4
              ◊ Q 6 2
              ♣ 10 9 8 7

♠ 8 5 4 2          N          ♠ K 6 3
♡ J 9                         ♡ A K Q 8 6 5
◊ A J 8 3     W  ✦  E         ◊ 9 7
♣ Q J 5            S          ♣ K 4

              ♠ A 10 7
              ♡ 3 2
              ◊ K 10 5 4
              ♣ A 6 3 2
```

"Rick was South and on lead against FOUR HEARTS. He led a trump. The declarer was Darryl, one of our clubs top players. Darryl won in dummy and led a club toward his king at trick two. Most of the Souths must have panicked at this point, fearing a spade discard on the clubs, and cashed their ace of spades...making four.

"Not Rick, though. He just led back a trump. There was nothing Darryl could do. He eventually led toward his spade king and lost two spades, a diamond and a club. Darryl couldn't believe it. 'What does everybody in this club do?' he moaned. 'Lead out their aces?'

"Here's another deal from the regional in Manchester." I drew a second deal on the pad.

```
                  ♠ J 7 6 4
                  ♥ J 9
                  ◊ K J 7 6
                  ♣ Q 7 6
  ♠ K 10 5              N              ♠ Q 2
  ♥ 8 4 3                              ♥ A K Q 7 6 5 2
  ◊ A 9 8 5 3      W  ⊹  E             ◊ 2
  ♣ J 4                                ♣ K 9 3
                       S
                  ♠ A 9 8 3
                  ♥ 10
                  ◊ Q 10 4
                  ♣ A 10 8 5 2
```

"I was South and on lead against FOUR HEARTS. As long as I don't lead my aces declarer can't avoid losing a spade and two clubs, and we get an above average board. If I ever cash my ace of clubs prematurely, declarer makes five."

I concluded my lesson by quoting George Buffon about genius and the virtue of patience (he must have had the handling of one's aces in mind!), and Matthew Granovetter in *Murder at the Bridge Table* who said that aces were meant to capture kings.

"Very interesting lesson," Claudia said.

This week at the club, however, I was South in the following deal:

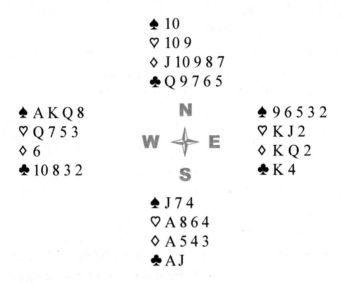

```
                    ♠ 10
                    ♡ 10 9
                    ◊ J 10 9 8 7
                    ♣ Q 9 7 6 5

♠ A K Q 8              N              ♠ 9 6 5 3 2
♡ Q 7 5 3                             ♡ K J 2
◊ 6            W  ─┼─  E              ◊ K Q 2
♣ 10 8 3 2             S              ♣ K 4

                    ♠ J 7 4
                    ♡ A 8 6 4
                    ◊ A 5 4 3
                    ♣ A J
```

After I opened ONE DIAMOND, East-West bid to FOUR SPADES. I led a trump. When I got in with the ace of diamonds, I returned a diamond. Then I got in with the ace of hearts. I couldn't stand it. Claudia just had to have the king of clubs, didn't she? I cashed the club ace! FOUR SPADES didn't make at any other table.

"I thought you taught me aces were meant to capture kings?" Claudia said sweetly.

"I know, I know." I said.

"How come you defend so great with all your other partners?" she asked. "Who was that Frenchman you quoted? Buffoon?"

"Buffon," I said. "George Buffon. Not Buffoon."

"Oh."

♠ ♡ ◇ ♣

# PART SIX
# Tournaments

So now you have been introduced to duplicate bridge. You've taken lessons to brush up on the game you used to play in college. You've practiced at home, and you've started playing at your local club.

Occasionally you got a good board or two, and even more rarely, you had a good game. You kept at it, though, buying books and reading, going over the hands after each session you played, discussing where you went wrong, and adding a convention or two to your arsenal, all the time striving to improve your bridge.

Then one night at the club, they passed out a flyer. There was a sectional tournament at the end of the month, or better yet, a regional. Some of the veteran club members noticed that you were an improving player interested in bettering your game, and they encouraged you to go. You were ready. It would be fun. Maybe someone even asked you to play in the Sunday Swiss.

What was that? They explained. Team bridge.

Are you ready? This is what you'd been working toward- to compete against other players from your section or region.

Do you remember your first tournament?

The last Saturday of the month arrives before you know it. The hotel lobby or the resort is all a bustle with folks going over their convention cards, signing up at the several registration tables, calling out to friends or acquaintances, or browsing through the wares at the book display. This is no little Mitchell game in a school cafeteria or a church hall. There are hundreds of bridge players here, and the excitement in the air is palpable.

You find the sign for the Flight C game, pay your entry and head for the appropriate ballroom. In a blur, you find your table, introduce yourselves to the other pair there, make the boards, pass them to the next table and get your boards, wish your opponents luck and take your cards.

It's tournament time!

♠ ♡ ◇ ♣

C H A P T E R  6 7

# The Flight C Blues

For those bridge players who do not remember what it was like to play in Flight C, or for those who were simply born Flight A'ers and never had to struggle to count to 13, here are a few reminders of what it is like looking up from the bottom of the bridge world.

In club games, there are the weekly encounters with folks who have been playing bridge for decades. Come tournament time, if the games are stratified, there is the pounding you have to endure at the hands of those in Flights B and A. On many a ride to a tournament with our friends Dave and Mary, who took up the game at roughly the same time Claudia and I did, the conversation would inevitably turn to those Flight A'ers. How did they get to be so good? Some of them were younger than we were. What kinds of minds must they have? Is it memory? Experience? An analytical mind? We've all read numerous bridge books, been faithful to the daily newspaper bridge column, and bid hundreds of Bridge World hands, yet we still look upon those A players with wonder and terror. Will we ever, ever be able to hold our own with them at the bridge table?

The worst part of being a C player, though, is the abuse we have suffered at the hands of the few A and B players who seem to go out of their way to give the game a bad name. David and Mary tell about one encounter with such a player who picked up their convention card to examine it before a round and laughed at it!

Claudia and I have had similar experiences. At a sectional tournament, we sat down against two top players. I picked up this hand with favorable vulnerability:

♠: A 6 3 2 ♡: K Q J 10 9 8 ◊: 5 2 ♣: A. I opened ONE HEART. ONE SPADE from LHO. TWO DIAMONDS from Claudia. TWO NO TRUMP from RHO. My hand was minimum and game was uncertain, but I could visualize a two trick set.

"What does her bid mean?" I asked LHO.

"Natural," he said.

I doubled.

PASS from LHO. THREE HEARTS from Claudia. Darn. She never trusted my doubles. I bid FOUR HEARTS and everyone passed. Here was the deal:

**DLR: SOUTH   VUL: E-W**

```
                     ♠ 7 4
                     ♡ 7 6 3
                     ◊ K J 10 9 4
                     ♣ K 9 4
   ♠ K J 10 9 5           N          ♠ Q 8
   ♡ 4                               ♡ A 5 2
   ◊ Q 8 7         W ─┼─ E           ◊ A 6 3
   ♣ Q 10 6 2          S             ♣ J 8 7 5 3
                     ♠ A 6 3 2
                     ♡ K Q J 10 9 8
                     ◊ 5 2
                     ♣ A
```

When Claudia tabled the dummy, Ms. Curmudgeon on my right said, "Well at least I had my bid."

"Excuse me?" I said, not quite believing what I had heard.

"I said at least I had my bid," she repeated.

I was dumfounded.

"I don't think I've ever heard anything quite so rude at the bridge table," I said. Thinking back on it, I should have called the director on Ms. Curmudgeon, not only for her rudeness but for giving her partner information before the opening lead. You really have to have a bit of a thick skin in order to earn your stripes in the bridge world.

Perhaps Ms. Curmudgeon was so upset because she could foresee her fate. And perhaps she should have concentrated on her defense instead of on our bidding. I got a club lead and perforce took my ace. I then led a diamond. Ms. Curmudgeon could have made it much tougher on me by ducking her ace. If she did that, though, I would then pitch a spade on my king of clubs and lead a spade. The defense could then never prevent me from ruffing a spade for my tenth trick. Ms. Curmudgeon gave me an easy ride to eleven tricks, though, by taking her ace of diamonds and leading a second club. I duly pitched a spade, knocked out the ace of trumps, won the spade return, drew trumps, took the second diamond finesse and claimed losing only to the ace of trumps and the ace of diamonds.

FOUR HEARTS making five was worth a 9 1/2 on an 11 top. One small step for Flight C...

# CHAPTER 68
# Playing Up - Part I

*Look not thou down but up.*
- Robert Browning

A number of years ago, a top player gave us some advice. "Always play up," she said. She was playing with a relatively new player at the time, and she made him play in the highest flight or bracket available. "People like to play in the lowest flight possible," she said. "They're afraid of the better players, but playing against them is where you can really learn some bridge."

We were forced to take that advice on a recent trip to the West Coast. We'd had our fill of some of the most spectacular scenery in North America on a month long drive up from San Diego, so we decided to take in the Emerald Empire Regional in Eugene, Oregon, for the weekend. We arrived on Thursday night, and there was no room in the Stratified pairs, so it was either a side game or the A pairs for the evening session.

"No way," my wife Claudia said. I don't belong in the A's. Who did you say was playing here?"

"Just Paul Soloway and Grant Baze."

"Forget it."

"Come on. It'll be fun."

What we learned in the A game was that A players give gifts like all other bridge players and that aggressive bidding, steady play and a little luck can equal success. There were two sections of A's, and the boards were scored across both sections, so a top was a 17.

Early in the game, Claudia (West) picked up ♠: Q J 10 6 2 ♡: K ◇: A 8 6 2 ♣: Q J 5 in third position. I passed and South opened ONE CLUB. Claudia overcalled ONE SPADE, and North bid ONE NO TRUMP. After two passes Claudia, undaunted, bid TWO SPADES. She doesn't usually rebid five-card suits, but I assumed it was her nervousness that made her do it. Here was the full deal:

**DLR: EAST**      **VUL: N-S**

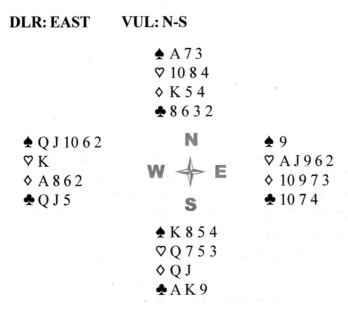

```
                    ♠ A 7 3
                    ♡ 10 8 4
                    ◇ K 5 4
                    ♣ 8 6 3 2

  ♠ Q J 10 6 2                      ♠ 9
  ♡ K                               ♡ A J 9 6 2
  ◇ A 8 6 2                         ◇ 10 9 7 3
  ♣ Q J 5                           ♣ 10 7 4

                    ♠ K 8 5 4
                    ♡ Q 7 5 3
                    ◇ Q J
                    ♣ A K 9
```

North made the unfortunate lead of the ten of hearts (top of nothing). As you can see, Claudia should lose two clubs, two diamonds, and two spades. She covered the heart ten with the jack, however, and South played his queen which Claudia won. Incredibly when South won the spade king, he continued hearts (apparently playing his partner for short-ness) and Claudia pitched two of her clubs on the ace and nine of hearts.

She now led a low diamond, won her ace and led the queen of spades. North won his ace, cashed the king of diamonds- dropping his partner's other honor- and gave his partner a ruff. South cashed the king of clubs and when Claudia's queen of clubs dropped, got out with a spade. An incredible plus 110 gave us a 15 on the board.

On the very next board:

229

**DLR: SOUTH    VUL: EAST-WEST**

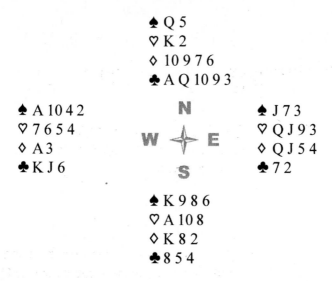

```
                    ♠ Q 5
                    ♡ K 2
                    ◊ 10 9 7 6
                    ♣ A Q 10 9 3

♠ A 10 4 2           N            ♠ J 7 3
♡ 7 6 5 4                         ♡ Q J 9 3
◊ A 3          W  -+-  E          ◊ Q J 5 4
♣ K J 6                           ♣ 7 2
                     S
                    ♠ K 9 8 6
                    ♡ A 10 8
                    ◊ K 8 2
                    ♣ 8 5 4
```

Claudia opened ONE CLUB with the West cards. I bid ONE DIA-MOND, she bid ONE HEART, and I raised to TWO HEARTS which ended the bidding.

North led the ten of diamonds, queen, king, ace. Claudia led a heart. North took his king and led another diamond. Claudia won and led the heart queen. South ducked, so Claudia left the ace out and led the jack of spades. North won his queen and exited with a spade (not best). Claudia scored two spades and a ruff, two diamonds, and a diamond ruff in her hand. She lost a spade, two hearts and two clubs. Making two for a 15 1/2.

Par on the hand was anywhere from 120 to 180 for N-S in no trump.

When we played these hands, we didn't realize how good our results were, so unbeknownst to us we were off to a pretty good start at the Emerald Empire Regional and our first attempt in Flight A.

♠ ♡ ◇ ♣

# CHAPTER 69
# Playing Up - Part II

*Challenge is a dragon with a gift in his*
*mouth...Tame the dragon and the gift is yours.*
- Noela Evans

So here we were in the Flight A game 3000 miles from home at the Emerald Empire Regional in Eugene, Oregon. We had long ago been advised to try playing in the A's because we would learn more about the game, but this was our first attempt. We had arrived in time for the Thursday evening session, but there was no room in the Stratified B-C game. In spite of Claudia's objections, I bought an entry for the second session of the A's.

Early in the session, Claudia made a couple of major suit partials when the opponents belonged in no trump, and we set a couple of slams when the opponents overbid. The only problem we were having was when Claudia arrived at each table and introduced us.

"Hi," she'd say. "We have no business playing in the A's. We should be playing in the B's but there wasn't any room."

I kept waving my hands and shaking my head whenever she did this. Finally between tables, I told her to stop making apologies. "They'll take advantage of us," I said. "Just act like we belong."

Later in the session, we got lucky in a couple of no-trump games.

**DLR: EAST    VUL: E-W**

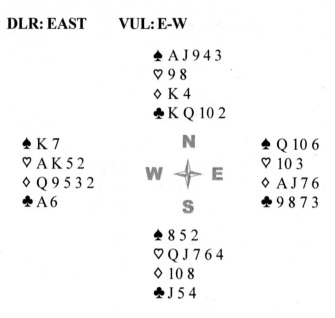

```
                    ♠ A J 9 4 3
                    ♡ 9 8
                    ◊ K 4
                    ♣ K Q 10 2

   ♠ K 7              N              ♠ Q 10 6
   ♡ A K 5 2                         ♡ 10 3
   ◊ Q 9 5 3 2    W  ✦  E            ◊ A J 7 6
   ♣ A 6                             ♣ 9 8 7 3
                    S

                    ♠ 8 5 2
                    ♡ Q J 7 6 4
                    ◊ 10 8
                    ♣ J 5 4
```

Claudia, West, opened ONE DIAMOND, North overcalled ONE SPADE, and I bid ONE NO TRUMP. Claudia invited with TWO NO TRUMP. I liked my ace and jack of diamonds, so I bid game. A club or a heart lead holds me to three. South, however, dutifully led his partner's suit. North took my king with his ace and returned a spade. I inserted the ten and now had ten tricks.

On the run of the diamonds, North erred and saved a spade instead of a club. South had also pitched a club. When I played the heart king, the ace and another club, North won and had to give me my queen of spades and good nine of clubs for eleven tricks and a 15 on the board.

We had the same kind of luck with this next game a few boards later.

**DLR: EAST**     **VUL: BOTH**

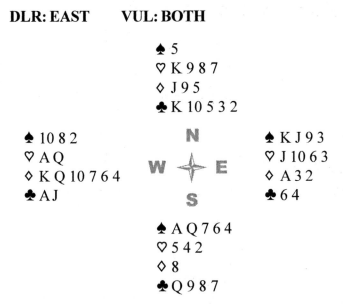

```
                    ♠ 5
                    ♡ K 9 8 7
                    ◊ J 9 5
                    ♣ K 10 5 3 2

   ♠ 10 8 2              N              ♠ K J 9 3
   ♡ A Q                               ♡ J 10 6 3
   ◊ K Q 10 7 6 4   W  ✦  E            ◊ A 3 2
   ♣ A J                 S             ♣ 6 4

                    ♠ A Q 7 6 4
                    ♡ 5 4 2
                    ◊ 8
                    ♣ Q 9 8 7
```

If West is declarer in no trump, she will get a club lead and go down. I, however, wound up declarer in THREE NO TRUMP and got a spade lead. I now had time to play the ace and queen of hearts. North, of course, should have ducked his heart king, but he took it and shifted to a club. That gave us eleven tricks and a 16 on the board. I guess the moral is if you're in Eugene and on opening lead against THREE NO TRUMP, lead a club!

We were thrilled to finish fourth in our section. My only disappointment (not Claudia's) was that we didn't run into Baze and Soloway. They were in the other section. We also went on to win the weekend knockouts with a team we picked up at the partnership desk. All in all not bad for an impromptu side trip. Now we were ready for the Columbia River Gorge, Mt. St. Helens and more spectacular scenery, but we would never forget our first attempt at playing up with the A's in Eugene, Oregon.

So, if you are aspiring to improve your bridge game and you find yourself at a tournament, don't be afraid of playing up. That flight A dragon just might be tamed, and then the gift in his mouth will be yours.

♠ ♡ ◇ ♣

# C H A P T E R  7 0
# The Other Table

*It is a mystery, containing, like all mysteries, the*
*possibility of torment.*
- James Baldwin

Swiss teams and knockouts are two of the more entertaining
formats in bridge.  For newer players, these team games can
also be much less stressful than playing in pairs.

In pairs, you must concentrate on every card.  Knowing whether
your seven of clubs is good at trick ten can be the difference between a
top and a bottom. Overtricks can spell either triumph or disaster.  Not so
in a team game. As declarer, you simply have to make your contract. As
a defender, it is no big deal if you make an aggressive lead and give up an
overtrick. Defeating the contract is your top priority.

The most fascinating aspect of teams is the mystery of what's happening at the other table.  You can seldom predict what is going on there.
Here is a case in point:

**DLR: EAST**　　**VUL: NONE**

```
                    ♠ Q 5 4
                    ♡ A Q 10 5 4
                    ◇ 10 4 3 2
                    ♣ J
        ♠ 8 7              N        ♠ 10 9
        ♡ K 9 8 7                   ♡ J 6
        ◇ 9 7 6 5      W   E        ◇ J 8
        ♣ Q 10 9          S        ♣ A K 8 7 6 5 4
                    ♠ A K J 6 3 2
                    ♡ 3 2
                    ◇ A K Q
                    ♣ 3 2
```

234

Playing in a Swiss Teams match, East opened THREE CLUBS. I bid THREE SPADES with the South hand and partner raised me to game. Six is cold, of course, and we worried that our opponents might have bid the slam. When we got to this board during the comparison with our teammates, I said quietly, "Plus 480." Our teammates were a couple from New Jersey that we had met at the partnership desk.

"Minus 2000," the man said with nonchalance as if this were a perfectly normal result.

I couldn't resist. "Minus 2000," I said, stunned. "What happened?"

"I meant to open THREE CLUBS," the man continued, "but I accidentally said THREE SPADES instead. South doubled and North alerted that it was for penalty. West and North both passed, and I, still not realizing what I had done, passed as well."

"Yes," the woman said. "When I put dummy down, I put my two spades on the left. 'No, no,' he tells me gruffly, 'the trumps go on the left.' But dear, I said, spades are trumps. You opened THREE SPADES."

"I took one trick," the man said. "Minus 2000. Sorry about that."

Of course, there are times when YOU are the other table. At a regional tournament, our teammates in knockouts came back to our table and proudly announced that on one board they had made five diamonds doubled and vulnerable only to discover that we had lost 13 IMPS on the deal and it had gotten us knocked out. Here's what happened. As South, I picked up an innocent looking:

♠: A K 9  ♡: J 10 9 8 7  ◊: Q  ♣: A 8 7 2

I opened ONE HEART. West doubled and East bid ONE SPADE. I bid TWO CLUBS and West bid TWO DIAMONDS. East bid TWO SPADES and West jumped to SIX DIAMONDS! I, somewhat insulted, doubled and my partner dutifully led a spade...the 7 of spades. Here is what I saw:

```
        N            ♠ Q 5 3 2
    W  ─┼─  E        ♡ 3 2
        S            ◊ 10
                     ♣ K 9 6 5 4 3

                  ♠ A K 9
                  ♡ J 10 9 8 7
                  ◊ Q
                  ♣ A 8 7 2
```

I played my king and chuckled at East's second bid of TWO SPADES. How could he have done that? West must want to strangle him. West, however, was a good player, and I should not have assumed he had lost his mind when he bid SIX DIAMONDS. Without realizing that a 2040 IMP swing was riding on my next card, I played the ace of spades. Making six! Here was the entire deal:

```
                  ♠ J 10 8 7 6
                  ♡ Q 6
                  ◊ 9 8 7
                  ♣ Q J 10

    ♠ 4                N            ♠ Q 5 3 2
    ♡ A K 5 4                       ♡ 3 2
    ◊ A K J 6 5 4 3 2  W  ─┼─  E    ◊ 10
    ♣ —                S            ♣ K 9 6 5 4 3

                  ♠ A K 9
                  ♡ J 10 9 8 7
                  ◊ Q
                  ♣ A 8 7 2
```

Declarer played his ace and king of hearts and ruffed a heart. He then pitched his last heart on the spade queen. The result would have been the same if I had tried to cash my ace of clubs. A heart return would have given us a one trick set while returning my "worthless" queen of diamonds would have resulted in down two as long as I held onto three hearts when declarer ran his diamonds. Why had I been in such a hurry to beat this "impossible" contract? Of course, I tried to pass the blame for this disaster on to partner.

"Why didn't you lead your spade jack?" I asked.

"I'm not the one who doubled," partner said. "Don't blame me. I would have led the queen of clubs if you hadn't doubled."

"Plus 750," our partners said proudly during the comparison when the round was over.

"Minus 1540," I said tremulously.

"What? What happened? You let them make six?"

Oh, there's one more difference between teams and pairs I forgot to tell you about. Instead of only one person mad at you, now you have three!

# C H A P T E R   7 1
# In the Cards

*I am the master of my fate:I am the captain of my soul.*
- William Henley

We all like to think of ourselves as the masters of our fates...the captains of our exploits in the bridge wars. Our skills in declarer play and defense will sweep us to success. We've read our Watson and our Sheinwold, and now we expect to conquer the bridge world.

But as Frank Stewart says in his fine book *Better Bridge For the Advancing Player,* "the real world of bridge turns out to be a disillusionment. You win by guessing, just guessing. You win by watching somebody go down in a game so cold that icicles seem to hang from the cards."

Observe these deals from a regional tournament in Danvers, Mass. My brother-in-law Eric and I were in the second round of the Friday night knockouts. At the half of our match, we had a 13 IMP lead. It was still anybody's game. Early in the second half, I picked up: ♠: K ♡: Q J 10 ◇: J 10 9 8 5 ♣: A K J 10. I opened ONE DIAMOND. Eric bid ONE SPADE. I rebid TWO CLUBS. TWO DIAMONDS from Eric. It was then that I noticed that my ace of clubs was really the ace of spades! What should I do? I had a balanced 15 points...I should have opened ONE NO TRUMP. Would Eric know what I was doing if I bid TWO NO TRUMP? We were vulnerable, and I decided that I couldn't chance it. I passed, and West led a spade. Alas, here was the whole deal:

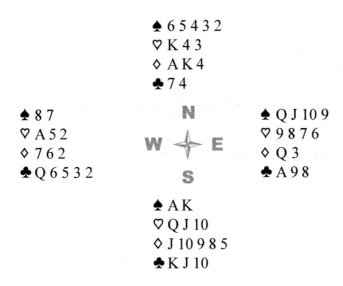

&spades; 6 5 4 3 2
&hearts; K 4 3
&diams; A K 4
&clubs; 7 4

&spades; 8 7　　　　　　　　　&spades; Q J 10 9
&hearts; A 5 2　　　　　　　　&hearts; 9 8 7 6
&diams; 7 6 2　　　　　　　　&diams; Q 3
&clubs; Q 6 5 3 2　　　　　　&clubs; A 9 8

&spades; A K
&hearts; Q J 10
&diams; J 10 9 8 5
&clubs; K J 10

I won the spade lead and led the jack of diamonds. When West didn't cover, I played the ace and king dropping the doubleton queen on my right. TWO DIAMONDS, making four. I was despondent and marked a ten IMP loss on my personal scorecard. We should have been in THREE NO TRUMP.

A couple of hands later, I was dealt: S: Q42 H: J943 D: Q764 C. 63. Eric opened ONE CLUB. East passed. Should I bid? I decided on ONE HEART. From Eric, TWO NO TRUMP. Oh, oh. I had done it again. I passed and squeamishly put down the dummy. East, however, had the ace of spades and the kings in the other three suits. Every time he led, he gave away a trick, so Eric made four. Should we have been in game? Eric had a funny look on his face.

We went to compare scores with our teammates. Had our lead held up? I didn't think so. The first three boards were pushes, then, "plus 130," I said painfully.

"Plus 200," our teammate said brightly. "Our opponents were in THREE NO TRUMP. We led a club. Declarer didn't guess the queen of diamonds doubleton and was down two!"

Another push, then, "plus 180," I said quietly.

"Plus 100," our teammate intoned. "We beat FOUR HEARTS one trick."

"Yeah," Eric said. "I didn't tell you. One of my hearts was mixed in with my diamonds. I had 19 points, and I would have jumped to FOUR HEARTS too if I had realized that I had four hearts."

We had held onto our lead and won the match. Our poor opponents, though. We had blundered our way to victory. Frank Stewart was right. Sometimes winning or losing is just in the cards- or at least in the cards you think you have!

♠ ♡ ◇ ♣

# Success

*Success is counted sweetest by those who ne'er succeed.*
- Emily Dickinson

S o how would you gauge your success as a bridge player? Have you worked at the game, taken lessons, played with better partners, subscribed to bridge magazines, built up your bridge library, and played bridge on line?

In spite of all this work, however, unless you are in the top echelon of bridge players, your success in this game is a very fragile thing indeed. You find yourself at the mercy of luck, fate, your finesses, your guesses, and either the skill or the gaffes of your opponents.

There are times when for no apparent reason you go on winning streaks when you can do no wrong and you think that you have finally arrived as a bridge player. Then, just as mysteriously, you plunge into one of bridge's black holes- a zone in which you can do nothing right, where every decision, every lead, every finesse, every bid is a disaster.

But, like the bowler striving for the perfect game, the golfer for that elusive hole in one, or the surfer for that one perfect wave, we press on in search of that next plateau in bridge where we will always make that textbook play, find that killing lead, that shift in time, or that perfect defense. Deep down there is the nagging feeling that we may never reach that plateau, that we have gone as far as we are going to go in bridge, but fortunately, this fickle, funny game keeps bringing us back for more where we are sustained by our partners and our (or their) sense of humor.

What time is next week's game?

♠ ♡ ◇ ♣

# CHAPTER 72
# The Black Hole - Part I

*Friends love misery in fact. Sometimes if we are
too successful...our misery is the only thing that
endears us to our friends.*
- Erica Jong

According to Stephen Hawking in his book *A Brief History of
Time- From the Big Bang to Black Holes*, the existence of
black holes in space was first suggested in 1783. A sufficiently massive
and compact star could have such a strong gravitational field that not even
light could escape. Everything would be sucked into this black void.

What Hawking didn't realize was that black holes also exist in bridge.
What is a bridge black hole? It is a losing streak so great, so profound,
that everything you do and everyone you play with gets sucked in. Every
bid you make is wrong, every opening lead a disaster. All of your partners
begin to behave bizarrely, sucked in by your negative gravitational field.
They, like you, become masters of the compression play turning ten
sure tricks into nine and going down in contracts that are ice cold.
Meanwhile your every opponent metamorphoses into a bridge genius,
bidding impeccably, defending devastatingly, and playing the dummy with
sheer artistry.

A black hole is no two or three game losing streak, no brief stretch of
bad luck. It is an abyss into which you plummet for weeks, so fathomless
and all-encompassing that every time you open a hand you wonder how
this one will blow up in your face.

Athletes today talk about being in "the zone" when they can do no
wrong, miss no shot. Well, I have known that feeling too, or rather its
inverse. When I am in "the hole," I and my partners can do no right.

242

Observe partner's defense on this deal when I was in "the hole." Partner had asked me to go to a sectional tournament. I tried to warn him away, tried to explain about the black hole, but he would hear none of it. This was the first board of the afternoon:

**DLR: SOUTH    VUL: N-S**

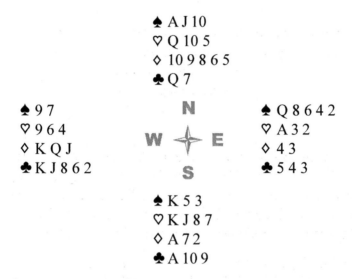

```
              ♠ A J 10
              ♡ Q 10 5
              ◊ 10 9 8 6 5
              ♣ Q 7

  ♠ 9 7           N          ♠ Q 8 6 4 2
  ♡ 9 6 4                    ♡ A 3 2
  ◊ K Q J      W ✦ E         ◊ 4 3
  ♣ K J 8 6 2      S         ♣ 5 4 3

              ♠ K 5 3
              ♡ K J 8 7
              ◊ A 7 2
              ♣ A 10 9
```

South opened ONE NO TRUMP, and North raised to THREE NO TRUMP. Partner led his king of diamonds, I played the three and declarer ducked. Partner ignored my card and the string of diamonds in dummy; doggedly he persisted with the queen. Declarer took this with the ace and, apparently in her own black hole, knocked out the ace of hearts. I won and returned a heart. Declarer then lost a spade finesse to my queen. I didn't have a diamond to return, so I tried a club and partner won his king. After some brief thought, he returned...a spade! What was he doing? Didn't he have the jack of diamonds- the setting trick? After declarer took her winners, there were three cards left in dummy- the ace of spades and the ten and nine of diamonds.

"I'm sorry partner," she moaned as she led a spade to her ace. "I should have shot back a diamond at trick three, and then I would have made this."

But wait. Partner hadn't played to the spade trick yet. He had a glassy look in his eyes. Incredibly, he discarded the diamond jack! Declarer, looking as though some governor had given her a reprieve, glee-fully took the last two tricks.

"What are you doing?" I exploded at partner. (Was this the big bang that Hawking was talking about?)

"Sorry," he said. "I completely forgot the queen of clubs had been played. I thought I would get thrown in with a diamond and have to lead away from my clubs. I was preventing an endplay."

My god. Partner had not accidentally pulled the wrong card. He had actually thought through this incredible play. I was about to tell partner that his logic made no sense whatsoever, but then I remembered. This wasn't his fault at all. He had simply been sucked into my black hole.

♠ ♡ ◇ ♣

# The Black Hole - Part II

*Formula for success: rise early, work hard, strike oil.*
- J. Paul Getty

Yes, I'm still in the black hole. In bridge, a black hole is a losing streak so great, so profound, that everything you do and everyone you play with gets sucked in.

Your partners, through no fault of their own, begin to exhibit bizarre behavior at the table. Remember my partner who not only didn't cash the setting trick at THREE NO TRUMP, he later threw it away so he wouldn't be endplayed!

The second characteristic of black holes is that your opponents become bridge geniuses as soon as they arrive at your table. If there is only one line of play that will bring home a thin game, your opponent will stumble into it. A killing defense against your game? You guessed it. I even had an opponent revoke once and then have to return a card he would have never otherwise played. That card was the only card in his hand that could have beat me.

If there are any of those unbiddable 21 point games out there, your opponents will get to your table, tell you they have been having a lousy session, and then with a shrug of their shoulders and a "what have we got to lose now?" attitude, they will bid it. Observe our opponents in action at a sectional tournament on this deal:

**DLR: NORTH   VUL: N-S**

```
                   ♠ A K Q J 3
                   ♡ K 8 5 2
                   ◊ 7 6 4
                   ♣ Q
    ♠ 9 7 6 5          N          ♠ 2
    ♡ Q J                         ♡ 10 6 3
    ◊ A 10 9 3     W  ✦  E        ◊ K Q 8 5 2
    ♣ K 7 6            S          ♣ A 9 4 3
                   ♠ 10 8 4
                   ♡ A 9 7 4
                   ◊ J
                   ♣ J 10 8 5 2
```

As the bridge gods are my witness, this was the bidding. North opened ONE SPADE. South bid ONE NO TRUMP. From North, TWO HEARTS. From South, THREE CLUBS! North tried THREE SPADES, and South ended this incredible auction with FOUR SPADES. I knew we were in trouble when South tabled the dummy and North beamed. "Thank you very much, partner," she said.

I, sitting East, led the king of diamonds, and the game came rolling home. This hand was played thirteen times, and our opponents were the only ones in game. I know, I know, if I lead my two of spades, declarer doesn't have an easy time of it, but I'm not in the habit of leading singleton trumps.

Then, in the evening session of the same tournament, along came two older gentlemen and this deal:

**DLR: NORTH   VUL: E-W**

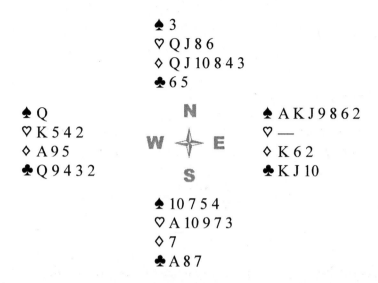

♠ 3
♡ Q J 8 6
◊ Q J 10 8 4 3
♣ 6 5

♠ Q
♡ K 5 4 2
◊ A 9 5
♣ Q 9 4 3 2

♠ A K J 9 8 6 2
♡ —
◊ K 6 2
♣ K J 10

♠ 10 7 5 4
♡ A 10 9 7 3
◊ 7
♣ A 8 7

When you are in a black hole, LOMS (little old men) can be just as formidable as LOLS (little old ladies). I was South on this deal. Try to imagine yourself as West watching your partner's bidding on this deal. North passed and East opened ONE CLUB! He later explained to his partner that he did this because he wanted to be sure that the hand was played in spades! I bid a slightly eccentric TWO CLUBS, a Michael's Cue Bid. West asked my partner what this meant, and he explained that I was 5-5 in the majors with 11-15 points. West bid THREE CLUBS. THREE HEARTS from my partner, and East contributed a perplexing bid of FOUR SPADES. I passed, and partner gave me a funny look. A befuddled West again asked my partner what my cue bid meant.

"He has five hearts and five spades, then?" asked West

"Yes," said my partner, that was our agreement.

West reached for he bid box and placed the FIVE CLUBS bid on the table. Partner passed. East looked at his cards for a moment and then bid SIX SPADES! Partner looked stupidly at me when I quickly passed and did not double. West stared hopelessly at his cards.

"I've been playing bridge for 30 years, and I have never seen bidding like this," he said shrugging and placing his PASS card on the table with an expression that said his partner had certainly lost his mind and there was nothing else that could be done for him.

Of course, you can look back at this deal and see what happened. Chalk up another zero for us. Partner was in shock, but he managed one last question.

"Black hole?" he asked.

"You've got it," I said.

♠ ♡ ◇ ♣

# The Black Hole - Part III

*He was a self-made man who owed his lack of success to nobody.*
- Joseph Heller

Help! I'm still in the black hole. Do you think Star Fleet Command has sent anyone out to look for me yet?

Black holes in bridge, remember, are losing streaks that are so long, so total, they assume an almost mystical aura. I have had fellow players tell me that they were in one of my black holes.

"Oh yeah," I said skeptically, "how many times have you been below average?"

"Twice. Everything has gone wrong for the last two sessions. It's awful."

I just smile. Twice! That's no black hole. Once you have been sucked into one of these bad streaks, your last average game- just an average- is a distant and bittersweet memory.

Let's review the characteristics of a black hole so you'll know if it's happening to you. Your partners begin to make inexplicably bizarre bids and plays. Your opponents metamorphose into bridge geniuses when they arrive at your table. Any decisions they make will inevitably turn out right. Every hand you open has the potential of blowing up in your face. A session of bridge becomes a walk through a minefield. When you're in a black hole and you pick up a hand, your first thought is, "I wonder what will go wrong this time."

Observe this devilish deal from the depths of one of my recent holes. In second position, I held: ♠: Q 7 ♡: A K Q ◇: K Q J 8 3 2 ♣: J 6. RHO opened ONE HEART. I overcalled TWO DIAMONDS. TWO HEARTS from LHO. Partner and RHO passed. Undaunted, I bid THREE DIAMONDS. From LHO, THREE HEARTS. North thought for a moment and then raised to FOUR HEARTS! How insulting. I doubled and led the king of diamonds. Here was the entire fiendish layout:

**DLR: NORTH    VUL: E-W**

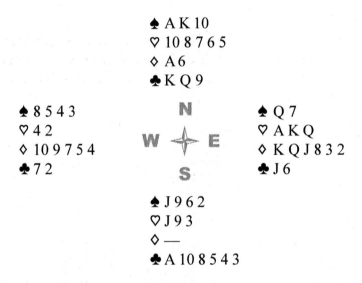

```
                      ♠ A K 10
                      ♡ 10 8 7 6 5
                      ◇ A 6
                      ♣ K Q 9

    ♠ 8 5 4 3              N              ♠ Q 7
    ♡ 4 2                                 ♡ A K Q
    ◇ 10 9 7 5 4      W  ✦  E            ◇ K Q J 8 3 2
    ♣ 7 2                 S               ♣ J 6

                      ♠ J 9 6 2
                      ♡ J 9 3
                      ◇ —
                      ♣ A 10 8 5 4 3
```

Notice that if North carelessly discards from dummy instead of ruffing my opening lead and then leads a trump, I can set him. But remember, this was my black hole. North's play was up to his bidding. Four hearts doubled, making four.

All right, so forget that one. A zero is a zero is a zero. Smile. Ignore partner's helpless and battered look. Next deal. Both vulnerable, I picked up:

♠: 6 5 3 ♡: K 4 2 ◇: 6 5 3 2 ♣: A K Q

It looked innocent enough, didn't it? I was in fourth seat. Three passes to me. What would you do? My hands began to tremble. Should I pass with three quick tricks? I tried to remember *Five Weeks to Winning Bridge*, the first bridge book I had ever read. What would Sheinwold say? What would my wife Claudia say? This was my black hole, don't forget. Whatever I did would blow up in my face.

I struggled to recall what I have forever known as Charlotte's rule. Charlotte, a charming older lady who had been playing bridge for many years when Claudia and I first encountered her at the bridge table, once told us that in fourth position you add your total points to your total number of spades. If the number doesn't add up to fifteen, you don't open—the theory being that if you open without spades, the opponents can then introduce and outbid you with the highest ranking suit. Well, this added up to 15, didn't it? Didn't it?

I opened ONE DIAMOND. Partner bid ONE HEART, and I ended the bidding with ONE NO TRUMP. The opponents were ominously quiet. LHO led a spade, and I fearfully waited for partner to lay down the dummy. Here was the entire layout:

**DLR: WEST      VUL: N-S**

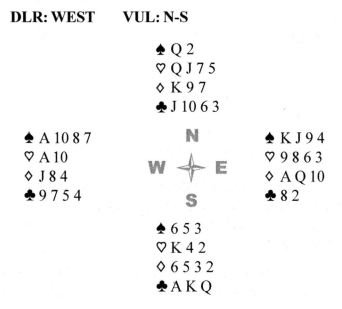

```
                    ♠ Q 2
                    ♡ Q J 7 5
                    ◇ K 9 7
                    ♣ J 10 6 3
   ♠ A 10 8 7          N          ♠ K J 9 4
   ♡ A 10                          ♡ 9 8 6 3
   ◇ J 8 4        W  ✦  E          ◇ A Q 10
   ♣ 9 7 5 4          S            ♣ 8 2
                    ♠ 6 5 3
                    ♡ K 4 2
                    ◇ 6 5 3 2
                    ♣ A K Q
```

When the opponents were done with me, I was -200. They took four spades, three diamonds, a heart, and no prisoners. At most tables, East-West were in TWO SPADES making an innocuous 110. Two tables were passed out. As my partner wearily wrote our score on the score slip, East nodded congenially to me.

251

"Say," he said, "I know you. You're the young fella who went to the finesse counselor, aren't you?"

"Yep, that's me."

"I know someone else you might be interested in. He's a hand evaluation therapist. Here's his card."

HELLLLP!

♠ ♡ ◇ ♣

C H A P T E R    7 5

# Comeuppance

*Thus the whirligig of time brings in his revenges.*
- William Shakespeare "Twelfth Night"

"Comeuppance," a punishment or retribution that one deserves, is one of science fiction writer Ray Bradbury's favorite words. Many people don't realize that the young Bradbury was hired by film director John Huston to write the screenplay for the 1956 adaptation of Moby Dick. Huston and Bradbury worked together on the project in Ireland, and it was the supercilious director's overbearing treatment of the young writer that prompted Bradbury to write a ghost story in which John Huston was done in by an Irish banshee.

"Comeuppance," Bradbury says with a smile on his face as he fondly recalls the story he wrote many years later in which the John Huston character receives his just deserts. "That's a great word, eh?"

Sometimes at the bridge table you have to be just as patient as Bradbury was to dish out your comeuppance. Case in point:

A number of years ago, I was playing in a Manchester, New Hampshire, Regional with Bob Clements, a fine player and eventual state champion. Our opponents for one round were Darryl Legassie and Jerrie Will from our local club in Dover, NH, and one of the top pairs in the state. It would have been great fun to do well against them, but along came this deal:

**DLR: NORTH    VUL: N-S**

```
              ♠ K 5
              ♥ Q J 5
              ◊ 10 8 2
              ♣ A K 10 8 7

♠ Q 8                          ♠ A 9 3
♥ A K 10 9 3                   ♥ 7 6 2
◊ A 6                          ◊ K Q 9 3
♣ Q 9 6 4                      ♣ J 5 2

              ♠ J 10 7 6 4 2
              ♥ 8 4
              ◊ J 7 5 4
              ♣ 3
```

Darryl, sitting West, arrived in the doomed contract of FOUR HEARTS after Bob, who was North, opened ONE CLUB, and I, sitting South, weak jump-shifted to TWO SPADES. Ha! My weak jump shift had gotten the opponents too high. Little did I know, however, that it would result in something else entirely. Bob was on lead, and as you can see, Darryl would lose the ace and king of clubs, a club ruff, and a heart. Not Darryl, though. Bob led the club ace, I perforce played my singleton three, and Darryl dropped...the queen!

"You dog, Darryl," I thought. "That's not a singleton. Come on, Bob, think! How many clubs would that leave me with? Why couldn't I have had the singleton 9? What else can you do, Bob? Continue!"

My psychic entreaties went unheeded, however, and unfortunately Bob did think of something else to do. He switched to...the king of spades. Nooo! Darryl made quick work of the hand, losing two clubs and a heart, making four. Darryl and Jerrie went on to win the Flight A pairs that year, getting a nice boost from this board, which shot Bob and me into a tailspin toward oblivion.

I have never forgotten that hand and Darryl's fine falsecard. It took many years for Darryl to get his comeuppance, and it took my wife Claudia to dish it out for me. Claudia and I were playing Darryl and Jerrie recently at our club when this hand came up:

**DLR: NORTH　VUL: NONE**

```
                    ♠ J 3
                    ♡ 4 2
                    ◊ A J 10 7 6 4
                    ♣ K J 8
  ♠ A K 9 7 4         N          ♠ Q 10 6 2
  ♡ J 10 9                        ♡ K 8 7 6
  ◊ 9 2          W  ✦  E          ◊ K 8 5
  ♣ A 7 4            S            ♣ 6 5
                    ♠ 8 5
                    ♡ A Q 5 3
                    ◊ Q 3
                    ♣ Q 10 9 3 2
```

Claudia, North, opened a weak TWO DIAMONDS. Darryl, East, passed. I, knowing the opponents had spades, furthered the preempt with THREE DIAMONDS.

This did its job, for Jerrie, sitting West, didn't think she had enough to come in at the three level, so this was passed out.

Her judgment was accurate, for THREE SPADES by East-West goes down one and FOUR SPADES down two as long as North leads her doubleton heart and gets a heart ruff. So everyone our way was either +50 or +100, and the pressure was on Claudia to get a plus score.

Darryl led the 6 of clubs. Claudia played low from dummy, and Jerrie gave her play a great deal of thought. She hated to catch defensive air with her ace, but finally she played the ace of clubs. Without a flinch, Claudia coolly dropped...the king of clubs!

Jerrie understandably switched to diamonds, and this rode around to the queen. Claudia continued diamonds. Why wasn't she pitching a spade or heart loser on her club queen?

You see, I was just as fooled as Jerrie was by the falsecard. Claudia lost a diamond, a club, and two spades, making three for +110 and a top!

"Was there anything I could have done?" Jerrie asked her partner.

"Well yeah," said Darryl. "You could have given me my club ruff."

Ah, comeuppance. Great word, eh?